KB139930

Diversity and Plurality among Muslims of North Africa

* This work was supported by the Ministry of Education of the Republic of Korea and the National Research Foundation of Korea (NRF-2018S1A6A3A02022221).

Diversity and Plurality among Muslims of North Africa

Mona Farouk M. Ahmed

Introduction

Being a Muslim from Egypt, I've often encountered misunderstandings when interacting with individuals from various backgrounds or different faiths. The root cause of these misconceptions often lies in the tendency to jump to conclusions through generalizations and preconceived stereotypes associated with Muslims. A prevalent misconception revolves around the notion that Muslims form a monolithic entity, sharing identical beliefs and attitudes. However, this perception is overly simplistic and fails to capture the intricacies of the Muslim community, which comprises roughly a quarter of the global population. It's crucial to recognize the diverse perspectives, practices, and cultural nuances that enrich the tapestry of the Muslim world. And this was simply the main purpose of this book to highlight this truth.

Are Muslims a monolithic group, or is there a range of beliefs among them? Is diversity and plurality present among them? These are some of the questions that this book seeks to answer, with a specific focus on the Muslim population of the North African region. The book's title briefly captures its core theme delving into the diversity and plurality among North African Muslims. With a comprehensive approach, the book commences by discussing the conceptual underpinnings of diversity and plurality, setting the groundwork for subsequent chapters. The introductory section in chapter one is dedicated to examining these very concepts within the broader context of global Islam, where various races, languages, cultures, and sects interplay to manifest the diverse tapestry of the Muslim world. In this light, the initial chapter comprehensively explores how plurality and diversity intricately shape the collective identity of Muslims worldwide.

The simple definition for plurality would be "a number greater than one" indicating being numerous.[1] Thus, plurality means having a various kinds with a large number. Conversely, a basic interpretation of "diversity" could be "possessing distinct or dissimilar characteristics or situations".[2] As a result, we use the term "plurality" to depict something encompassing multiple groups, while we use "diversity" to emphasize its inclusion of varied individuals from diverse social and ethnic backgrounds, along with differing genders, sexual orientations, and more.

Applying these terms on the Muslim groups of the world, we can see

---

1 See the definition of "plurality" in the dictionary: https://www.dictionary.com/browse/plurality

2 See the definition of "diversity" in the Oxford English dictionary: https://www.oed.com/search/dictionary/?scope=Entries&q=Diversity

that they are numerous and cannot be simply categorized as a single entity. The Muslim world consists of a multitude of sects, many of which further branch into sub-sects. Among these groups, diversity is also evident in various aspects, including races, cultures, and languages. This is simply the main idea of the book to highlight this plurality and diversity in one of the regions of the Muslim world.

Sunni, Shi'a, Ibadi, and Ahmadiya serve as prominent examples of the numerous Muslim sects. Alongside these, there are also groups such as Sufi, Salafi, secular, and Qur'ani, which may intersect within these sects. In addition to other many Islamist groups involved with politics including the group of Muslim brotherhood which has a universal presence extending in many countries including Egypt and Palestine. There are also extremist Islamist militant groups who adopted terror like Al-Qaeda, and ISIS. Hence, the global Muslim community comprises a multitude of groups, each characterized by distinct principles and attitudes.

Delving into the region of North Africa, the diversity seen in the region was discussed in the second chapter. This diversity includes the richness of cultures, identities, and ethnicities in this region. Arab, Muslim, Berber, and African are examples of this diverse identities found in North Africa composing its cultural richness reflected in its arts, literature, architecture, foods, and other cultural aspects. Also, geographical diversity was discussed as it has its impact on shaping the culture and economy of the region. Other aspects of diversity introduced in this part of the book was the religious diversity which may not be noticed at the first impression as Islam is the dominant religion in all the countries of North Africa. But, examining deeply the religious status in those counties we can see the religious diversity and plurality through its history and at present as well.

The book focus on each of the North African countries starting with Egypt in chapter three under the title of "Diversity of Muslims in Egypt: contradictions and paradoxes" exploring the different Muslim groups found in Egypt and discussing their relations which include some interesting contradictions and paradoxes. Within the spectrum of Egyptian Muslim groups, Salafis and Sufis have critical relations marked by many tensions between them. In addition to these groups, there is a large Muslim population that does not align itself with any particular religious group. They can be categorized as non-denominational Muslims. Many of them chose to be just Muslims with no additional affiliation to avoid splitting and divisions within the Muslim community. Alternatively, some are influenced by their lack of knowledge due to their ignorance and illiteracy. Carelessness also was among this choice for some Muslims who, merely by name, identify themselves as Muslims due to ancestral inheritance and conformity to the prevailing societal norms.

As for Libya, chapter four focused on the tribal plurality among Muslims in Libya introducing the variety of tribes in this North African country. The rich tapestry of tribal diversity that characterizes Libyan society becomes evident as the country is divided into five regions, hosting over a hundred tribes with different origins and distinct traditions. The prevalent tribal composition in Libya is dominated by two major categories: Arab tribes and Arab-Berber tribes. These groups hold sway over the majority of the northern and central regions of the country, forming a significant cultural and demographic presence. Additionally, their influence extends to certain pockets within the southeastern Kufra region. Libya is also home to many non-Arab native tribes. Noteworthy examples include the Amazigh, Tuareg, and Tebu tribes. These indigenous groups contribute to the rich tapestry of Libyan society, showcasing the diverse and multifaceted nature of the country's tribal landscape.

Hence, the Libyan scenario vividly portrays the prevalence of plurality and diversity within the realm of tribalism among the Muslim population in North Africa. This portrayal offers valuable insights that address the core inquiries posed by this study, as presented within the pages of this book.

Chapter five focused on the so-called Islamist groups with their political role in Algeria. Alongside these factions, numerous non-Islamist groups also actively contribute to the enhancement of Algerian society, wherein a Muslim majority prevails. The exploration of the dynamic between Islamism and secularism in this North African nation highlights a protracted conflict between the Algerian authorities and Islamist entities, which has left a discernible impact on the societal landscape of Algeria.

This analysis brings to light yet another layer of the multitude and diversity that characterize the Muslim population within this particular region. By delving into the intricate interactions between Islamist and secular forces in Algeria, it becomes evident that the landscape is rich with various ideological and sociopolitical currents. This complexity underscores the varied perspectives and trajectories that Muslims in this area navigate, reflecting the diverse tapestry of beliefs and affiliations that shape their collective identity.

The application of Islamic concepts is likewise characterized by a range of diverse understandings and interpretations. This phenomenon becomes particularly evident when examining the situation in Tunisia. This aspect is underscored by the focus of chapter six, which thoroughly explores the evolution of Islamic concepts within the Tunisian context, tracing their transformation across the spectrum of tradition and modernity.

The transformation of Islamic concepts in Tunisia finds its roots in the impact of successive secular governments that have held authority from the nation's attainment of independence up until the 2011 revolution. Consequently, Tunisian governance has inclined towards curtailing religious fundamentalism through a series of measures and policies. This trajectory underscores how the interplay between state governance and religious interpretation has shaped the development of Islamic notions in the Tunisian context.

Incorporating these dynamics introduces additional layers of diversity to the intricate fabric of North African Muslims. The Tunisian society, characterized by its distinctive approach to implementing Islamic concepts, stands out as a vivid example of this complex panorama. The diverse interpretations of Islamic principles within the Tunisian context further enrich the nuanced array of viewpoints and identities that shape the Muslim landscape across the region.

Examining the mystical dimension of Islam, Sufism also has given rise to a wide array of diversity and plurality through the spread of numerous Sufi groups across the Islamic world. Specifically, Morocco give a good example for this plurality and diversity of Sufi groups composing a large sector of the global Muslim community. Chapter seven introduced another aspect of diversity found among Muslims of North Africa focusing on the plurality and diversity of Sufi groups in Morocco.

Within Morocco, thousands of Sufi institutions, including zawiyas, ribats, and shrines, hosting various Sufi groups hail from distinct Sufi orders. These groups actively enrich Moroccan society, assuming pivotal roles within the nation's social and political framework. The spiritual facets of Sufism have profoundly resonated with the Moroccan populace, fostering a sense of spiritual resilience and societal cohesion.

Although Sufism faces criticism for its hierarchical nature from some Muslims, it thrives with the support of governments in many countries, including Morocco. Confronting the modern challenges, Sufism endures as a strong force, skillfully adapting to changing circumstances while staying true to its foundational principles within the Moroccan context. This wide array of Sufi institutions offers a diverse range of activities customized to align with their traditions and the requirements of their followers.

Finally, as a conclusion of the book, challenges and future prospects on the diversity of Muslims in North Africa were derived through a combination of descriptive analysis and the historical approach used in this research proving the rich diversity and multifaceted nature of North African Muslims. By highlighting the intricate tapestry of Muslim identities and experiences in the North African region, this work establishes a solid foundation for a deeper understanding of the cultural, historical, and socio-religious dynamics at play. These derived insights would provide guideposts for navigating the complex landscape of diversity among North African Muslims, offering direction and potential pathways to address pressing challenges and seize opportunities for growth and inclusivity.

Mona Farouk M. Ahmed
Busan, South Korea
On 30 September 2023

contents

Chapter 1

Exploring the Diversity and
Plurality Among the Muslims of the World

I. The concept of plurality and diversity in Islam

The two concepts of "plurality" and "diversity" are so related, as "plurality" reflects the presence of multiple distinct elements within a larger context while "diversity" refers to the variety of those elements. Thus, in this chapter, examining these two concepts regarding Islam will be focusing on answering questions about how Islam sees the plurality and diversity of mankind and how far these concepts are reflected in the Muslim world today.

The human plurality was respected in Islam from the early beginning of the Quran revelation as the Islam prophet was sent not only to his people like other prophets but to all worlds. The equality among people based on their belief in God was stressed in many verses including this verse, which confirms the plurality and diversity of mankind while dedicating that the nobility among people is based on their obedience to God: "O humankind We [God] have created you male and female, and made you into communities and tribes, so that you may know one another. Surely the noblest amongst you in the sight of God is the most God-fearing of you. God is All-Knowing and All-Aware" (Quran 49:13). This Quranic verse summarized the concept of plurality according to the Islamic view referring to the natural aspect of plurality and diversity seen in the human community which should stimulate the curiosity of people to earn more knowledge about each other and thus enriching the human relations.

According to Islam, other faiths also are respected and Muslims should respect other people's beliefs as there is no enforcement of religion according to Islamic teaching confirmed in Quran. This can be seen in many examples of Quran verses including the vivid verse saying: "Let there be no compulsion in religion, for the truth stands out clearly from falsehood" (2:256). Chapter 109 of the Quran called "the disbelievers" summarizes this issue simply in a short verse addressed to the disbelievers: "You have your way, and I have my Way" (Quran 109:6). Thus, Muslim society according to the Islamic teachings accept the religious plurality within the respect of other beliefs unless aggression occurred by the others against Muslims.

In this chapter, we will explore diversity and plurality with its wide aspects among the Muslims of the world in general while examining the different sects of Islam at present.

II. Aspects of Plurality in Muslim communities

The relations between Muslims and the main Abrahamic religions of Christianity and Jews are organized according to the Islamic concept recognizing Christians and Jews as the people of the book.[1] According to this concept, intermarriage that is allowed between Muslim men and women of Christians and Jews, added religious plurality to many Muslim families throughout history.

Religious plurality was also expected to happen among the Muslims which is seen in the various Muslim sects spread throughout history. This was clear in Quran addressing the prophet: "Indeed, you ⌜O Prophet⌟ are not responsible whatsoever for those who have divided their faith and split into sects. Their judgment rests only with Allah. And He will inform them of what they used to do" (Quran 6:159). Thus, the plurality of Muslim sects also was expected like other religions. Seeing that Islamic teaching is promoting respecting other beliefs as long as they respect Muslim beliefs, so Muslims should also respect the beliefs of other Muslims as their affair is up to God who is the only one who owns the

---

1 Calling them the people of the book is based on the Islamic belief that they received the holy book of God through their prophets as Muslims believe in all the messengers of God including all the Jewish messengers and Jesus as well.

right of judging people of their beliefs.

Theoretically, this is the case. But, in reality, not all people are rational enough to peacefully coexist with people of other beliefs, especially when this is involved with political and economic interests. That is why we can see the persecutions of others leading to wars and conflicts throughout history.

% of population
Muslim

90–100
80–90
65–80
50–65
30–50
15–30
7–15
1–7

Source: (Hunter, 2014)

Fig. 1: Map of the Muslim distribution in the world

A quick view of the map in Fig. 1 can prove the variety and plurality of Muslim communities in the world today. It shows that Muslims are distributed with different percentages all over the world including different races, languages, and cultures. The African continent shows more concentration of Muslims especially in its northern part, while the Muslim populations in Asia cover the South West in the origin point of Islam in the Arabian Peninsula where the Muslim community expanded to the surrounding regions in addition to the southeast of Asia where Indonesia has the largest Muslim population in the world.

Examining the largest Muslim population in the world, the first five countries are not Arab as after Indonesia with its 231 million Muslim population as for the statistics of 2021, the second place for the largest Muslim population is in Pakistan with over 2 hundred million of Muslims. Ironically, the third place is not even a Muslim country! As the third largest Muslim community is in India with a number of 2 hundred million Muslims. The fourth largest Muslim population is in Bangladesh, a Muslim country with a majority of more than 150 million Muslims. The Fifth place is for Nigeria, the African country with about 100 million Muslims (World Population Review, 2022). Then Egypt, Iran, and Turkey follow respectively adding to the variety of the Muslims of the world with their distinctive cultural background reminding of the ancient Egyptians, the Persian Empire, and the Turks with their contributions to world history and civilization melted into the Islamic civilization forming their large Muslim communities today.

III. Diversity of races in the Muslim world

The wide expansion of the Muslim population all over the world started from the small cities of Mecca and Medina in the Arabian Peninsula in the seventh century to reach China of Asia in the east and the Iberian Peninsula of Europe in the west under the Muslim rule in some periods of the history as seen in the map of Fig. 2 showing the Muslim world gradually expanding from the seventh century to cover a vast area in the middle of the world by the ninth century. This expansion was under the rule of different Muslim kingdoms with various races including Arabs, Turks, Mongols, Kurdish, and other races of the founders of many Muslim kingdoms spreading Islam into other lands of the world. Accordingly, the Islamic world expanded over lands of former kingdoms including the Persian and Roman Empires which were the greatest of that time. Naturally, culture plurality and diversity formed the Muslim nation composed of a large variety of races and cultures of peoples who adopted Islam under Muslim rule or due to the contacts with Muslim traders and travelers since the emergence of Islam.

The map in Fig. 2 shows the expansion of Muslim rule from its emergence in the seventh century till its most expansion during the ninth century under the Abbasid Caliphate. We can see from this map that the Muslim territories expanded to cover the Central Asian lands and to reach the Chinese and Indian borders in the east under the Abbasid Caliphate, while the rule of the Umayyad Caliphate reached France's borders in Europe through the Iberian Peninsula.

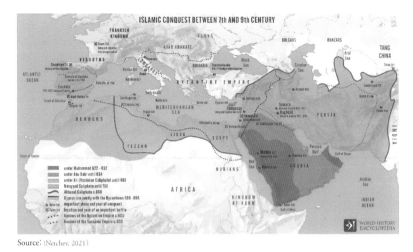

Source: (Netchev, 2021)

Fig. 2: Map of the Muslim Expansion in the world(7th -9th century)

The Muslim conquest was not the only way of spreading Islam, as there are countries that adopted Islam without being conquered by Muslims. In this context, we can mention some examples like Indonesia, Malaysia, Nigeria, and Maldives where Islam emerged peacefully due to the contact with Muslim travelers and traders. Muslim migration into many places all over the world also contributed to the spread of Islam in many countries and the emergence of new generations of Muslim minorities in those countries including the far continents of the two Americas and Australia.

IV. Lingual diversity

In Islam, lingual diversity is a natural phenomenon among humankind and one of the Divine signs. The Quran verses show appreciation for the diversity of languages stating that: "And among His Signs is the creation of the heavens and the earth, and the variations in your languages and your colors: verily in that are signs for those who know." (Quran 30: 22).

This Islamic interpretation of lingual diversity differs from Judaism and Christianity seeing that the Hebrew Bible states that the first language of men used by Adam was the only perfect one, but it was lost when the Babylonians started building a city with a high tower to reach the heavens. Thus, to prevent communication among those builders so that to stop their plan, God made them lose that perfect language and scattered them into different multi-lingual communities. Similarly, in Christianity, this idea was developed by interpreting lingual diversity as a curse proving the confusion of humans (Khan, 2009, p. 74).

The long history of Muslim rule over those wide territories had its impacts on the people of those lands contacting with Muslim Arabs and other races under the Islamic umbrella. These impacts can be seen in many cultural aspects including languages, traditions, arts, and architecture. The inter contacts and cultural exchange melted the peoples of those regions forming their new culture with a mixture of diversity. Many Arab words found in languages like Turkish, Spanish, Persian, Urdu, and Kurdish are examples of this cultural exchange, as those languages also had their influences on the Arabic language especially forming the modern Arabic dialects with many words of those languages.

Today's Muslim world has the richness of lingual diversity seen in the multi-lingual communities composing that world while commonly respecting the Arabic language. Unavoidably, the influence of Arabic on the Muslims with their different origins is notable seeing that Arabic is the language of the holy Muslim book "The Quran", which all Muslims should recite in their five prayers daily, and they believe it is the words of God used for his worshiping. Thus, Muslims learn at least basic Arabic to read the Quran. Moreover, some languages gave up their original alphabets and used Arabic scripts like the Urdu (Spoken in Pakistan), Persian (used in Iran, Afghanistan, and some other central Asian countries), and Hausa (used in some African countries like Nigeria).

Today, the Muslim world is composed of many communities extending all over the world with many Muslims maintaining their native tongues for many centuries. With the rise of the nation-states, preserving the national features including the language was stressed to highlight that diversity of those Muslim communities. Among those Muslims preserving their language and national identity, some are struggling for their independence like the case of Kurds living in Iran, Turkey, Iraq, and Syria. Another example can be seen in Pakistan, a multi-lingual Muslim country with Urdu as the national language, while its eastern part speaking the Bangla language that is not spoken in the rest of Pakistan was separated establishing Bangladesh stating its national identity seen in its name meaning "the home of Bangla" (Khan, 2009, p. 79).

Preserving the national language may imply struggle and face difficulties. Even some people lost their mother tongue within a few generations due to lingual policies or other factors including immigration. The lingual policies can be seen in the concept of the official language as its adoption may imply intolerance of other languages. An example of the changing lingual policies can be seen in Turkey where the Turkish language formerly used many Persian and Arabic words under the Muslim Ottoman rule, while the new government in Modern secular Turkey adopted lingual policies to cleanse the Turkish language of those Arabic and Persian elements. Accordingly, the Latin alphabet replaced the Arabic script in 1928. Moreover, those policies imposing the Turkish language included issuing laws that discriminate against the Kurdish language (Khan, 2009, p. 85).

Briefly, we can say that the expansion of Islam included mostly an Arabization process spreading the Arabic language and Arabic culture in the conquered lands like the case of all Arab countries in North Africa at present. Accordingly, there are some countries that gave up their original languages under Muslim rule adopting Arabic. However, Arabic was not always the language imposed by the rulers of Muslim countries as we can see in other cases including the Turkish language with a similar process called Turkification or Turkization emphasizing the Turkish culture and language.[2] Throughout history, the language of the ruler used to be

---

2   In this context, for more details on the Turkification of Kurds under Ottoman rule, see: (Tas, 2014. p. 43).

promoted by the people under his rule. Examining ancient and medieval history, we can see that the religion also of the ruler was imposed on his people. The lingual policies usually accompanied those religious policies seen in the Christianization often accompanied by Latinization similar to the case of Islamization accompanied by Arabization.

As the present is inextricably linked to the past, the current linguistic diversity of the Muslim world today can be understood within its historical context beginning with the Arab conquest of non-Arab lands and developing through the promotion and toleration of other languages by non-Arab Muslim rulers. This development was facilitated by other means of peaceful transmission of Islam, such as preaching, trade, travel, intermarriage, and immigration, which resulted in a more lingual variety of people adopting Islam.

V. Diversity of the cultural blending

The Muslim World expands today over many countries of different cultural roots including Indians, Chinese, Central Asians, Africans, Egyptians, Turks, Persians, etc. Adopting Islam as a religion does not mean abandoning the cultural legacies especially when it has no violation of Islam. Thus, the pre-Islamic cultural heritage of the Muslims had its influence on forming their culture in the modern era. This can be seen in the formation of the various Arabic dialects influenced by the original languages of peoples like the Amazigh of North Africa. Examining the Moroccan, Algerian, and Tunisian dialects of Arabic shows many examples of this influence of the Amazigh language called Tamazight.[3]

In some cases, we can even find some customs rooted in the pre-Islamic cultures that differ from the Islamic traditions. In this context, we can mention the influence of the Ancient Egyptian culture in the design of graves for burying the dead. According to the Islamic tradition, the "Lahd" is the usual form for burials. "Lahd" is a lateral hollow dug into the side of the grave ceilinged with raw bricks. But in Egypt, there are many graves without this "Lahd". Instead, the common design for most of them consists of underground rooms for burials. This difference led to debates among Muslim scholars as some of them see it violating the Islamic rules for burials. However, the Egyptian Dar Al-Iftaa, which is the official foundation authorized for giving fatwas in Egypt, had explained that it is permissible to bury in those Egyptian burials as long as they are well-sealed to prevent the emanation of odor and so that to protect it from being dug by animals (The Egyptian Dar Al-Ifta).

Cultural blending is not only seen from region to region or country to country in the Muslim world but it is also seen inside the same country in many cases. Multiculturalism is a phenomenon that is seen

---

3 In this context, there is some research showed the influence of Tamazight in Moroccan Arabic concluding that the Amazigh language has deeply impacted the structure of Moroccan Arabic through its grammar, phonetics, morphology, and phonology. See: (Lahrouchi, 2018).

in many Muslim countries due to many factors gathering people of various cultures to live together. The long foreign rule and immigration can be seen among those factors that contributed to this phenomenon. The technological revolution in modern time opened the doors widely on cultural interaction, as today the internet breaks the borders among countries and gives people great opportunities for meeting and exchanging their thoughts and cultural experiences. The cloth fashions, the ethnic and international cuisine, the new arts, and all other cultural elements spread the world widely across the internet with its social networks. Not only are the people of the Muslim world influenced culturally by those global trends since it is hard to be culturally isolated in the world today.

VI. Diversity of Muslim Sects

Religion like any other human culture has various aspects and a wide range of concepts that differs through times, peoples, and places. That's why we find various groups within the same religion. Islam is one of those religions that faced the same fate of the different understandings and misunderstandings of humans.

It was even predicted in Islam from the beginning that there will be various groups within the Muslim community that even will lead to disputes and conflicts among them. Some Quranic verses explain this human nature of diversity and that people split into sects having different religious concepts as stated in this Quranic verse: "Had your Lord willed, He could have made humanity one community, but they continue to differ" (11:118).

Examining the Muslim sects in the world today, we can see that among them the two major groups are the Sunni and Shi'a dividing also into many sub-groups. The Sunni sect is considered by many the "orthodox" branch of Islam composing the majority of Muslims in the world. The Shi'a group is concentrated basically in Iran and is considered the second-largest sect in Islam, as Shi'a Muslims constitute about 10-13% of the world's Muslim population (Blanchard, 2006, p. 1). The Ibadi sect is the third Muslim sect according to the timeline of the emergence of Muslim sects. The similarity between Ibadi and Sunni sects made them seen sometimes as one sect (Blanchard, 2006, p. 5). Historically the Shi'a sect emerged supporting the right of Prophet Mohamed's family and his descendants in the leadership of the Islamic nation. Accordingly, the political context regarding the Muslim leadership witnessed significant incidents that deepened the dispute between Sunni and Shi'a sects, especially with the death of the prophet's grandson Hussein which remarks one of the tragedies of this disputes (Upal & Cusack, 2021, p. 179). The Ibadi sect developed from the Khawarij sect that emerged during the first disputes among Shi'a and Sunni sects over the Islamic leadership since the Seventh century. However, the Ibadis do not admit their relations with the

Khawarij. For Ibadis, the Muslim leadership should be decided based on knowledge and piety regardless of race or lineage (Hoffman, 2022).

Source: (DinajGao, 2010)

Fig. 3: Distribution of the Sunni, Shi'a, and Ibadi sects in the Muslim world

The map of Fig. 3 shows the distribution of these three sects in the Muslim world. Through the map, we can see that the Shi'a sect is represented mainly in Iran with about 40%, Pakistan, India, and Iraq. Actually, the Shi'a Muslims are represented as the majority in Iran, Azerbaijan, Bahrain, and Iraq. Other Shi'a populations can be found with sizable numbers in countries like Turkey, Yemen, Azerbaijan, Afghanistan, Syria, Saudi Arabia, Lebanon, Nigeria, and Tanzania.[4] The Ibadi sect is centered mostly in Oman as seen on the map but also found in some

---

4 For more information about those numbers: (Pew Research Center, 2009)

parts of East Africa, Algeria, Libya, and Tunisia. As seen in the map (Fig. 3), the dominant Islamic sect is the Sunni sect covers the rest of the Islamic world.

There are more sects developed throughout history among Muslims. Al-Ahmadiyya sect is one of those sects denied by other Muslim sects. Moreover, inside Sunni and Shi'a sects, there are sub-divisions as summarized through the following figure (Fig. 4).

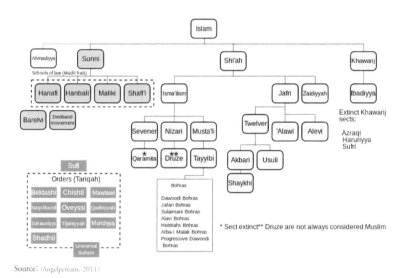

Source: (Angelpeream, 2011)

Fig. 4: Main Muslim Sects and sub-sects

Sufism can be considered a large sect, although it's not a distinct sect, as it's existed in the 2 main Muslim sects of Sunni and Shia. In that sense, Sufism can be defined as a mystic and ascetic aspect of Islam, it is considered as the part of Islamic teaching that deals with the purification of the inner self by focusing on the spiritual aspects of religion.

Another classification that can be applied to any religion in the world would include Conservative, Liberal, and Innovative groups. Thus, Muslims of the world regardless of their Islamic sect also varied according to their attitudes and personal beliefs.

For me, as a Muslim I can classify Muslims based on my witnesses in Muslim societies to the following:

Non-denominational Muslims: Even within Sunni or Shi'a sect many Muslims actually don't belong to any denomination. Sometimes, this is because of their lack of knowledge about Islam, which is understandable seeing the percentage of illiteracy in the Islamic world. Others studied Islam well enough to decide to refuse sectarianism and prefer to unite all Muslims under the name of just being Muslims without denominations.

Conservative Muslims believe that all the Qur'an and (usually) the Hadith traditions are for all times, except for parts specifically abrogated. They mostly try to follow the lifestyle and traditions of the prophets and the first Muslims of the prophet companions while rejecting almost all other traditions if not adopted by those first Muslim generations.

Liberal Muslims want a changed, mellowed-down Islam adapted to their modern lifestyle. Some of them read the Qur'an adopting new explanations matching the modern times. Some of them do not pray five times a day or fast during Ramadan. They mostly ignore what the Hadiths say about Muslim women having to wear veils. Some even drink alcohol and do not care about eating Halal food.

Innovative groups have strange theology that is different from the Qur'an. An example of those groups can be found in the Nation of Islam (Black Muslim group) taught the black race was superior and the white race was created by devils. But, actually many groups especially those of the extremist conservative Muslims judge other Muslim groups as innovative groups according to their principles based on following the same traditions of the first Muslim generations without changing them, so they judge many new habits and modern traditions as innovations against the right Islam.

In short, we can see through this chapter that the Islamic world is reflecting a wide range of variety and plurality reflected in the different races, languages, cultures, and sects representing the Muslim population all over the world today.

▪ References

Angelperearn. (2011, Jan. 31). *Islam branches and schools.* Retrieved from Wikipedia: https://ko.wikipedia.org/wiki/%EC%9D%B4%EC%8A%AC%EB%9E%8 C%EA%B5%90#/media/%ED%8C%8C%EC%9D%BC:Islam_branches_ and_schools.svg

Blanchard, C. M. (2006). *Islam: Sunnis and Shiites.* Washington: Congressional Research Service, The Library of Congress.

DinajGao. (2010, Feb 1). *Map of predominantly Sunni or Shi'a regions in the world.* Retrieved from Wikimedia: https://commons.wikimedia.org/wiki/ File:Sunni-Shi%27a_map.png

Hoffman, V. J. (2022, Aug. 12). *Ibadi Islam: An Introduction.* Retrieved from I Illinois University Library: https://guides.library.illinois.edu/ c.php?g=348315&p=2347041

Hunter, M. T. (2014, June 29). Islam percent population in each nation World Map Muslim data by Pew Research. *Wikimedia Commons.*

Khan, A. (2009). Protection of Languages and Self-Expressions under Islamic Law. *Journal of Transnational Law & Policy, 19*(1), 61-122.

Lahrouchi, M. (2018). The Amazigh influence on Moroccan Arabic: Phonological and morphological borrowing. *International Journal of Arabic Linguistics, 4*(1), 39-58.

Netchev, S. (2021, June 8). *Islamic Conquests between the 7th-9th Centuries.* Retrieved from World History Encyclopedia: https://www.worldhistory.org/ image/14212/islamic-conquests-in-the-7th-9th-centuries/

Pew Research Center. (2009, Oct. 7). *Mapping the Global Muslim Population.* Retrieved from Pew Research Center's Forum on Religion & Public Life : https://www.pewresearch.org/religion/2009/10/07/mapping-the-global-muslim-population/

Tas, L. (2014). *Legal Pluralism in Action: Dispute Resolution and the Kurdish Peace Committee*. New York: Routledge.

The Egyptian Dar Al-Ifta. (n.d.). *What is the correct way to burry the dead and the correct shape of graves?* Retrieved from Dar Al-Ifta Al-Missriyyah: https://www.dar-alifta.org/Foreign/ViewFatwa.aspx?ID=6964

Upal, M. A., & Cusack, C. M. (2021). *Handbook of Islamic Sects and Movements*. Leiden: Brill.

World Population Review. (2022). *Muslim Population by Country 2022*. Retrieved from World Population Review: https://worldpopulationreview.com/country-rankings/muslim-population-by-country

Chapter 2

Uncovering the North African Diversity

The North African region, as indicated by its name, refers to its location in the northernmost part of the African continent. It encompasses several countries, including Algeria, Egypt, Libya, Morocco, and Tunisia, which will be the focus of this book. Geographically, as depicted in Figure 1, the region is defined by its proximity to the Mediterranean Sea in the north and the vast Sahara Desert in the south.

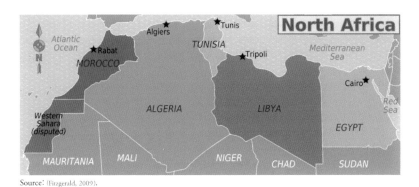

Source: (Fitzgerald, 2009).

Fig. 1: Map of the North African Region

From the east, the region is bordered by the Red Sea, and from the west, it is border by the Atlantic Ocean.

I. Diverse Identities in North Africa:

The richness of cultures, ethnicities, and other historical elements contributed to the diversity of the North African identities including Arab, Muslim, Berber, and African identities. The population of North Africa is primarily composed of Arabs, Berbers (Amazigh), and various ethnic groups of African origins including Nubians of South Egypt, Tuareg of the Sahara Desert, and Toubou of Libya.[1] Thus, one of the most significant aspects of North Africa's diversity is its ethnic makeup. Each of those ethnic groups has a distinct culture and also a distinct language preserved to add more plurality and diversity to the region.

As for religious identity, Islam is the main religion adopted in North Africa since the Arab Muslim Conquest in the seventh century starting with Egypt and gradually was expanded towards the west conquering Libya, Tunisia, Algeria, and Morocco applying an Arabization process with the Islamization of the whole region. However, other religious minorities exist in North Africa including Christians and Jews. In this context, the region has a long history of religious coexistence, with

---

1 For more information about those ethnic groups, see: (Hassouba, 2015), (Zerrougui, 2010), (Gérard, 2012).

followers of different faiths including some traditional African and ancient beliefs still influencing religious life today.

As an Egyptian, through my eyewitnesses, I can mention some ancient traditions still Egyptian Muslims preserve regardless of their religion. The method of burying the dead mentioned in Chapter one is an example. Also, Egyptians still celebrate ancient pre-Islamic feasts like "Sham El-Nesim" which means in English "smelling the breeze" referring to the good weather of the spring season. Other pre-Islamic traditions include celebrating the newborn babies on their seventh day of birth, commemorating the dead on the 40th day after their death, and using some ancient Egyptian amulets to prevent envy and devils. These are all non-Islamic traditions still preserved by Egyptian society today.

Linguistically, North Africa is also diverse. Besides the officially used Arabic, there are many languages widely used by the North Africans including Berber, French, and other languages spoken across the region. The diversity can be seen even within each language with a variety of dialects. Examining the Arabic dialects, we can distinguish clear differences among those Arabic dialects starting with Egyptian in which we can find influences of other languages like Turkish and ancient Egyptian languages, and ending with the Moroccan dialect rich with Berber, Spanish, and French words.

Based on this diversity rooted in the North African people, it is understandable to see this region rich in cultural diversity, which is reflected in its arts, literature, architecture, foods, and other cultural aspects. The cultural heritage of North Africa can be seen as a result of a complex exchange of influences among the indigenous peoples and other peoples settled in the region including Arab, Turkish, Spanish, French, and British people. In this context, the influence of colonialism is one of the factors that contributed to this cultural diversity. The long period of colonialism would have produced blended culture influenced by the culture of the colonizer. This point will be covered in more detail in a later part of this chapter.

North Africa is a region with a rich and diverse cultural heritage, with a wide range of ethnic, religious, and linguistic groups. Some of the major ethnic groups in the region include the Berbers, who have lived in the area for thousands of years, as well as Arabs and sub-Saharan Africans. These groups have different languages, customs, and traditions, which have all contributed to the cultural mosaic of the region. The diversity of identities seen in North Africa have created societies with diverse and rich culture, but also led to various forms of cultural, ethnic, and religious conflicts. The Berber uprisings in Algeria in the 1980s and 1990s, tensions between the Nubians and the Egyptian government after their displacement due to the construction of the Aswan High Dam in the 1960s, and more recently, the 2011 Libyan civil war are examples of those conflicts.[2] Thus, differences among the groups within the diversity

---

2 For more details, see: (Selim T. H., 2010), (Kleinbauer, 1978), (Harchaoui, 2017).

sometimes led to conflicts arising.

Examining this issue related to the identity closer in one of the North African countries, we can see that in Algeria all Algerians are almost of a Berber origin as about 99% of the Algerian population are Arab Berber Today. Despite this fact, only a few of them (about 15%) forming a minority are identifying themselves as primarily Berber. Those Berbers have long struggled and sometimes violently for their autonomy which is rejected by the Algerian government accepts only the official recognition of the Berber languages (CIA, 2023).

Actually, the term "Berber" is not accepted by the Berber community as it bears colonial influence. The French used this term to call the Maghreb's indigenous people, and earlier Romans were the first who used this word to refer to the non-Latins as "Barbaros" meaning "barbarians" in English. Accordingly, Amazigh, which means "the free people" is the preferred term for Berbers to identify themselves. They have their own flag which was banned in several incidents by the Algerian government arresting people who wave that flag for the crime of threatening national unity (Cheref, 2020). The picture in Fig. 2 shows the Amazigh flag called "Yaz".

The Amazigh or Berbers who were among the indigenous peoples living in North Africa would summarize the issue of identity in the region as they are mostly seen as Arabs now using the Arabic language and influenced by the Arabic culture while only minorities of them

Source: (Amazigh World, n.d.).

Fig. 2: The Amazigh Flag

persist on their original identity. Other factors such as Islamization and later westernization had impacts on their identity as well as adding more diversity to their culture.

II. The Geographical Mosaic of North Africa

The North African region is not only rich in its cultural diversity, it is also rich in its geographical diversity. Naturally, North Africa is a region that is characterized by its varied geography, which includes a variety of different landscapes. Logically, the geographical diversity would have its impact on shaping the culture and economy of the region, as well as influencing the distribution of its populations and the diversity of its natural resources.

The term "mosaic" usually refers to the combination of different elements that together form a unique and complex whole. Applying this term to the geographical landscape of North Africa, we can see this clearly in the different geographical features of North Africa including deserts, coastal regions, plateaus, mountains, river valleys, and oases, appearing like pieces of a mosaic that come together to form a unique varied landscape. An overlook of the geography of North Africa would show us this diversity through the following division of the region:

a) Deserts cover large lands of North Africa. We can see that much of the Sahara Desert known as the largest hot desert in the world is located in North Africa. This desert is also known for its vast sand dunes, rocky plateaus, and oases, and it covers large parts of Egypt, Libya, Tunisia, and Algeria. Even deserts have diversity in North Africa that can be seen in their various appearance as in the white desert and the black deserts of Egypt. See the unique appearance of those deserts shown in the pictures in Fig. 2.

The black desert   The white desert

Source: (Abdelrahman, Bahariya Oasis of Egypt, 2022)   Source: (Abdelrahman, Bahariya Oasis in Egypt, 2022)

Fig. 2: The black desert and the white deserts in Egypt

b) Oases are another unique type of geographical feature found in deserts. North Africa is rich with those Oasis found in the Sahara desert and other arid regions. These Oasis are characterized by a source of water, that allows vegetation to grow and thus sustain human settlements in the mid of deserts.

Source: (colceres, n.d.)

Fig. 3: The architecture of Siwa Oasis in Egypt

Siwa Oasis is one of those attractive spots for tourism in Egypt with its hot springs and the beauty of nature, in addition to the unique architecture seen in its buildings housing Berbers of Egypt. The picture in Fig. 3 shows this unique architecture in Siwa Oasis.

c) Coastal Regions as seen in the Mediterranean coast of North Africa characterized by mild temperatures, fertile soils, and abundant rainfall. This region is home to many important ports and cities, including Alexandria and Tunis. Not only the Mediterranean coast, but there are also other coastal regions on the red sea in the east of Egypt, and the Atlantic Ocean in Morocco which are rich with different features. The cities on the red sea in Egypt are famous of scuba diving attracting many tourists from all over the world for this sport as the Red Sea is well known for the beauty of its underwater life. Among those attractive spots for scuba diving is the blue hole in the city of Dahab located in the Sinai Peninsula in Egypt (Fig. 4).

Source: (Klavins, 2022)

Fig. 4: The blue hole of the Red Sea in the Egyptian city of Dahab

The coastal cities of North Africa are famous of resorts attracting tourists to enjoy the beauty of their beaches. The picture seen in Fig. 5 was taken from an airplane for the Egyptian city "Hurghada" located on the coast of the Red Sea and in a governorate named after the Red Sea. The picture shows Hurghada's resorts on the coast of the Red Sea.

Source: Picture taken by the Author.

Fig. 5: Resorts on the Red Sea in Hurghada, Egypt

d) High Plateaus and mountains are another geographical features of North Africa. They can be seen starting from the west of the region in the Atlas Mountains expanding on the lands of Morocco, Algeria, and Tunisia. In Lybia, we can see the Tibesti Mountains expanding to Chad and Niger and separating the coastal regions from the deserts. Another example can be seen in the mountains of Sinai and the mountains of the Red Sea in Egypt.

The Pictures in Fig. 6 summarize the diversity of those mountains shown in their different landscapes. They are characterized by rugged terrain, sparse vegetation, and cool temperatures that sometimes is snowing in winter. They are also rich in natural resources such as minerals including phosphate, iron, copper, and silver in the Atlas Mountains (Mikesell & İsnard, 2020). The Tibesti Mountain is also rich in minerals such as tungsten, tin, and oil in addition to large deposits of uranium (The Editors of Encyclopaedia, 2015).

Atlas Mountains in Morocco
Source: (D'Arby, 2018)

Mount Sinai in Egypt
Source: (Moustafa, 2014)

Fig. 6: Mountains in North Africa

e) Rivers and valleys are also found in North Africa including the Nile river of Egypt which is the longest river in Africa. Other examples of rivers in North Africa are the Kebir River in Algeria, the Mejerda River in Tunisia, the Wadi Draa River, and the Sebou River in Morocco. Rivers especially in the middle of the large North African deserts play an important role in providing irrigation for agriculture and allowing the formation of human settlements along the river throughout history. Ancient civilizations were established on rivers such as the ancient Egyptian civilization on the Nile River. In general, the river valleys in North Africa are known for their fertile soils and rich agricultural lands. These river valleys are the backbone of the agricultural economy of North Africa contributed to the formation of human settlements and civilizations in the region throughout history.

III. Western influence on North African diversity

Since the Muslim conquest of North Africa starting with Egypt in the seventh century, the region was gradually Arabized influenced by the Arab Muslim rule resulting in adding an Arabic identity to its countries now known as Arab countries among the 22 countries of the Arab league. Thus, for centuries the Arabic language and culture were rooted in the North African countries penetrating into its original cultures of Berber, Egyptian, and other African cultures. Actually, Berbers also succeeded to survive and to establish their kingdoms in some periods such as the Zirids, Hammadids, and Almoravids in the eleventh century.

By the end of medieval times, North Africa was under the control of the Ottoman Empire adding Turkish influence to the culture of the region. The weakness of this empire invited European colonization to

North Africa from the eighteenth century starting with the short period of the French occupation of Egypt in 1798 till 1801 followed later by a long British occupation that lasted from 1882 till 1954.[3] Then, France returned to the region capturing Algeria in 1830. And by the nineteenth century, only Morocco and Tunisia were independent until almost half of that century. In 1881, Tunis was under French protection. And later in 1912, the Moroccan protectorate was also established by France who soon divided the country with Spain. Thus, Spain also was invited to the political scene in North Africa taking control of the Rif Mountains and the border region. Similarly, Libya was by Italy in 1911. Eventually, by the time of World War II, North Africa was totally occupied by the European powers (Brett, n.d.). This was a quick brief on the history of Western colonization in North Africa. The long period of Western control would have its impacts on the society and culture of the region used to have mainly a Berber and Arab identity before.

Western education was another factor through which westernization of the North African societies took place. Usually, the colonizer imposes his culture and language, and that is what we can see in the western colonization of North Africa. France imposed its French culture through education in Algeria. Thus, until the independence of Algeria in 1962, French culture dominated Algerian education (Heggoy, 1973, p. 180). The

---

3 The Anglo-Egyptian treaty of 1954 ended the presence of the British armed forces in Egypt. For more information, see: (Selak, 1955).

impacts of this were strong enough to see that even today while the Arabic language is the official language of Algeria, Algerian universities are still teaching courses in French, especially for natural science subjects (Chachoua & Schoelen, 2019).

Politically, Many North African countries have adopted a form of government modeled after Western democracies. The Egyptian constitution is based upon the French Civil Code and other European codes besides Islamic law (Abdel Wahab, 2019). Economically, Western companies have invested in various industries including oil, gas, and mining in North Africa. ExxonMobil, Chevron, and Total are examples of famous companies investing in oil and gas exploration and production in North Africa, particularly in countries like Libya, Algeria, and Egypt. Siemens Gamesa, General Electric, and Total are also investing in solar and wind energy projects in North Africa.

The trade between North African countries and Western nations continues to increase, particularly, with France, Italy, and Spain. Mainly, North African countries export goods such as oil, gas, phosphates, textiles, and agricultural products to Europe, and import manufactured goods, machinery, and technologies. In this context, statistics showed that the increase of the EU exports of goods to North Africa from € 59 billion in 2011 to € 76 billion in 2021, with a steady growth rate of the imports from North Africa to the EU in the same period (Eurostat , 2022).

The importance of North Africa's exports to Europe can be clear by examining the oil exports of one of those North African countries to Europe. As for Libya, despite the small share contributed by this North African country to the world's supply of oil, 85 % of Libya's crude oil is exported to Europe, namely Italy and France heavily depend on Libyan oil and Gas as well (Yerkes & Hill, 2021).

The Western influence on North Africa is not only through the European countries with their history of colonization in African countries. The United States has a great influence can be seen in many aspects being a major trading partner with many North African countries as the U.S. imports oil and gas from countries like Algeria, Libya, and Egypt, and also imports agricultural products from North Africa. American military aid also is significant for the armed forces of the North African countries.[4]

Speaking about the western influence regarding the military field, the intervention of NATO in Libya in March 2011 was a quick response to violence that accompanied the regime change in Libya. But compared with the similar situation in Syria, this military intervention highlights the importance of Libya to Europe and confirmed the European direct interests in Libya (Isaac, 2012).

Other fields influenced by the west include tourism as one of the major sources of income for most North African countries. The financial

---

4 For more details, see: (Damis, 1985).

services provided by Western banks are also highly presented in North African countries. Western technology is also increasingly imported by North African countries. This can be seen in various sectors including telecommunications through Western companies such as Cisco, Vodafone, Orange, Ericsson, and Nokia. Also, many Western companies provide technology for the transportation sector in North Africa.

Western Media has a significant influence in North Africa as well. This can be seen by examining the popularity of the Western movies, television shows, songs, and music in North Africa which have an influence on the local media and film industry in the countries of the region.

Western Cuisine penetrated into the local taste of the North Africans through the worldwide famous chains, such as McDonald's and KFC with their restaurants in all North African countries. Italian pizza became so popular food for most North Africans through many international chains found in major cities of the region.

Those were just examples of the many fields through which the Western influence can be seen in North Africa which added more dimensions to its cultural diversity. It is worth noting that the influence cannot be always just a one-way direction, as the North African culture also has its impact on the West. The long contact implies the inter-exchange concept among regions.

IV. The diverse religious landscape of North Africa

The religious landscape of North Africa may give the first impression of non-diversity as Islam is the dominant religion in all the countries of North Africa. But, examining deeply the religious status in those counties we can see the religious diversity and plurality.

According to the statistics of the Pew Research Center, 93% of the population in North Africa and the Middle East are Muslims, and expected to increase to 93.7% by 2050. Besides Islam, within the rest of 7% of the North African population, 1% are Christians. Thus, the second Religion in North Africa is Christianity with the largest Christian communities found in Egypt, Tunisia, and Algeria (Pew Research Center, 2015, p. 154).

The vast majority of Muslims in North Africa belong to the Sunni sect. Other Muslim sects are present with few numbers in North African countries. For example, in Algeria, Sunni Muslims comprise more than 99% of the population. The rest 1% of the population includes other Muslim sects of Ibadi, Ahmadi, and Shia in addition to other religions of Christianity and Judaism (United States Department of State, 2016).

Christianity emerged in North Africa through Egypt where the holy family carrying Jesus the child was hosted after they fled from Palestine. In Alexandria, the first Catechetical school in the world was probably founded as early as 190 AD. Christian monasticism also was first founded in Egypt. And likely, the Egyptian priest Saint Anthony was the world's first Christian monk (Nmah, 2018, p. 10). Legends provided that Christianity was brought to Alexandria by Saint Mark of the four evangelists in 60 AD. Since then, Christianity spread from Egypt to other parts of Africa to reach Sub-Saharan Africa by the 15th century with the arrival of the Portuguese.

Egyptian Christians suffered persecution under Roman rule until the fourth century as the Roman Emperor Constantine adopted Christianity to become the official religion of the Roman Empire in 312. Gradually, different forms of Christianity developed resulting in diverse groups of Christians. The Church in Constantinople (Istanbul at present) as the center of the Roman Empire by that time, adopted the idea that God was both human (Jesus) and divine, which was not accepted by the Coptic church of North Africa adopting the Monophysite belief believing that God was one indivisible unity and wholly divine.

As for the Western regions of North Africa, more forms of Christianity, starting with the early movement of "Donatism",[5] and the diversity of churches developed later by the Western missionaries including the Presbyterian, Anglican, Evangelical Protestant, Catholic, and Orthodox.

Especially, since the 18th century, with the increasing European

---

5 Donatists named after their leader "Donatus" whom they supported against other Roman Catholics in the church bishop election were a Christian group that emerged in North Africa in 312 AD (The Editors of Encyclopaedia Britannica, 1998).

intervention into North Africa, we can examine the efforts of Western missionaries seeing many Protestant and Catholic organizations formed to promote Christianity and missionary work in the region, such as the Baptist Missionary Society, London Missionary Society, Church Missionary Society, and Religious Tract Society. These organizations were primarily led by English-speaking Protestants, but later joined by continental Protestants from Germany, Switzerland and France, as well as Catholic organizations such as Francis Libermann's Congregation of the Holy Ghost, Melchior de Marion-Bresillac's The Society of African Missions, and Society of Missionaries of Africa (White Fathers) which was founded to maintain a non-proselytizing presence among the Muslims and started in Algeria by its activities in the field of education during the years 1867-1868, to spread their activities then covering the Algerian Sahara and Tunisia by 1875 and soon reached other parts of Africa (Viera, 2007, pp. 250-251).

Even though Islam is the predominant religion in the region, North Africa is home to a diverse range of religious groups, including Christian minorities with various sects and divisions as above-explained. Other religions, such as Judaism, Bahaism, folk religions, Buddhism, and other religions[6] also relatively have very small communities but they are still

---

6 The 2012 statistics of the Pew Forum on Religion stated that there are some adherents of Buddhism, Hinduism, and folk religion with about 0.1% in each of the countries in North Africa (Hackett & Grim, 2012, pp. 45-50). For statistics about the number of adherents of religions in some

present. However, there is also a number of non-affiliated individuals or atheists which is uncertain due to social and political pressure to conceal one's religious identity. All this can be observed within the concept of "religious diversity" in North Africa.

countries of North Africa, see: (Office of International Religious Freedom, 2021), (Office of International Religious Freedom, 2022), (Office of International Religious Freedom, 2019).

▪ References

The Editors of Encyclopaedia Britannica . (1998, July 20). *Donatist.* Retrieved from Encyclopaedia Britannica : https://www.britannica.com/topic/Donatists

Abdel Wahab, M. S. (2019, Nov.). *An Overview of the Egyptian Legal System and Legal Research.* Retrieved from Hauser Global Law School Program, New York University School of Law: https://www.nyulawglobal.org/globalex/Egypt1. html#_The_Egyptian_Legal

Abdelrahman, I. (2022, April 15). *Bahariya Oasis in Egypt.* Retrieved from unsplash: https://unsplash.com/photos/zVUg0iaDzG8

Abdelrahman, I. (2022, Feb. 25). *Bahariya Oasis of Egypt.* Retrieved from unsplash: https://unsplash.com/photos/uQnXT5Blm1k

Amazigh World. (n.d.). Retrieved from Amazigh World: http://www.amazighworld. org/images2/Drapeau%20Amazigh%20gr.jpeg

BBC. (n.d.). *The Story of Africa: Christianity.* Retrieved from BBC: https://www.bbc. co.uk/worldservice/africa/features/storyofafrica/8chapter1.shtml

Brett, M. (n.d.). *North Africa after 1830.* Retrieved from Encyclopaedia Britannica: https://www.britannica.com/place/North-Africa/North-Africa-after-1830

Chachoua, K., & Schoelen, L. (2019, July 27). Higher Education Systems and Institutions, Algeria. In *Encyclopedia of International Higher Education Systems and Institutions.* Dordrecht: Springer. Retrieved from BBC: https:// doi.org/10.1007/978-94-017-9553-1_436-1

Cheref, A. (2020). *Don't call us Berber, we are Amazigh.* Retrieved from The National News: https://www.thenationalnews.com/opinion/comment/don-t-call-us-berber-we-are-amazigh-1.965334

CIA. (2023, Jan. 11). *The World Factbook: Algeria.* Retrieved from CIA: https://www. cia.gov/the-world-factbook/countries/algeria/

colcerex. (n.d.). *Siwa Oasis*. Retrieved from freeimages: https://www.freeimages.com/photo/siwa-oasis-1230758

Damis, J. (1985). United States Relations with North Africa. *North Africa, 84*(502), pp. 193-234.

D'Arby, T. (2018, April 17). *Ait Baha of Morocco: Green Trees on Brown Mountain.* Retrieved from pexels: https://www.pexels.com/photo/green-trees-on-brown-mountain-6739794/

Eurostat . (2022, Feb.). *Africa-EU - international trade in goods statistics.* Retrieved from Eurostat statistics: https://ec.europa.eu/eurostat/statistics-explained/index.php?title=Africa-EU_-_international_trade_in_goods_statistics&oldid=554854#Northern_Africa_largest_trade_in_goods_partner

Fitzgerald, P. (2009, March 11). *Contemporary political map of North Africa.* Retrieved from wikipedia: https://en.wikipedia.org/wiki/History_of_North_Africa#/media/File:North_Africa_regions_map.png

Gérard, M. (2012). *The Toubou of the Libyan Sahara: Historical, Anthropological and Development Aspects.* Leuven: Peeters Publishers.

Hackett, C., & Grim, B. J. (2012, Dec.). *The Global Religious Landscape.* Retrieved from The Pew Forum on Religion & Public Life: https://assets.pewresearch.org/wp-content/uploads/sites/11/2014/01/global-religion-full.pdf

Harchaoui, J. (2017). *Libya's civil war.* Washington, D.C.: Carnegie Endowment for International Peace.

Hassouba, M. (2015). The Nubian Pharaonic Civilization: An Historical and Cultural Overview. *Journal of African History, 56*(1), 1-28.

Heggoy, A. A. (1973). Education in French Algeria: An Essay on Cultural Conflict. *Comparative Education Review, 17*(2), 180-197.

Isaac, S. K. (2012). *NATO's Intervention in Libya: Assessment and Implications.* Retrieved from European Institute of the Mediterranean: https://www.

iemed.org/publication/natos-intervention-in-libya-assessment-and-implications/

Klavins, R. (2022, Aug. 11). *Underwater Tropical Corals Reef and sea fish Red Sea in Egypt Dahab Blue hole*. Retrieved from unsplash: https://unsplash.com/photos/yK_eIU3S40g

Kleinbauer, W. E. (1978). *Displacement and Resettlement in the Nubian Valley: The Aswan High Dam*. Washington D.C: The American Association for the Advancement of Science.

Mikesell, M. W., & İsnard, H. (2020, Feb. 20). *Atlas Mountains*. Retrieved from Encyclopedia Britannica: https://www.britannica.com/place/Atlas-Mountains

Moustafa, D. E. (2014, Oct. 17). *St. Katherine of Sinai*. Retrieved from unsplash: https://unsplash.com/photos/nXlUIwIaH84

Nmah, P. E. (2018). Christianity and Islamic Encounter in North Africa: Its Ambivalence. *UNIZIK Journal of Religion and Human Relations, 10*(1), 1-33.

Office of International Religious Freedom. (2019). *2019 Report on International Religious Freedom: Tunisia*. Retrieved from U.S. Department of State: https://www.state.gov/reports/2019-report-on-international-religious-freedom/tunisia/

Office of International Religious Freedom. (2021). *2021 Report on International Religious Freedom: Morocco*. Retrieved from U.S. Department of state: https://www.state.gov/reports/2021-report-on-international-religious-freedom/morocco/#:~:text=More%20than%2099%20percent%20of,Jews%2C%20and%20Baha'is.

Office of International Religious Freedom. (2022, June 2). *2021 Report on International Religious Freedom: Algeria*. Retrieved from U.S. Department of State: https://www.state.gov/reports/2021-report-on-international-religious-freedom/algeria/#:~:text=Religious%20Demography,Muslims%20following%20the%20Maliki%20school.

Pew Research Center. (2015, April 2). *The Future of World Religions: Population Growth Projections, 2010-2050*. Retrieved from Pew Research Center: https://assets.pewresearch.org/wp-content/uploads/sites/11/2015/03/PF_15.04.02_ProjectionsFullReport.pdf

Selak, C. (1955). The Suez Canal Base Agreement of 1954. *American Journal of International Law, 49*(4), 487-505. doi:10.2307/2194417

Selim, K. (Director). (1939). *Al-Azeema (The Will)* [Motion Picture]. Retrieved from https://www.dailymotion.com/video/x8ew3by

Selim, T. H. (2010). *Amazigh Activism in Algeria: The Rise of a New Ethnic Movement*. Berkeley: University of California Press.

The Editors of Encyclopaedia. (2015, Oct. 18). *Tibesti*. Retrieved from Encyclopedia Britannica: https://www.britannica.com/place/Tibesti

United States Department of State. (2016, Aug. 10). *2015 Report on International Religious Freedom - Algeria*. Retrieved from Refworld: https://www.refworld.org/docid/57add8ac15.html

Viera, P.-V. (2007). Christian Missions in Africa and Their Role in the Transformation of African Societies. *Asian and African Studies*, 249-260.

Yerkes, S., & Hill, T. (2021, Feb. 23). *A New Strategy for U.S. Engagement in North Africa: A Report of the North Africa Working Group*. Retrieved from Carnegie Endowment For International Peace: https://carnegieendowment.org/2021/02/23/new-strategy-for-u.s.-engagement-in-north-africa-report-of-north-africa-working-group-pub-83926

Zerrougui, A. (2010). *The Tuareg: A Culture in Transition*. New York: Algora Publishing.

Chapter 3

———

Diversity of Muslims in Egypt: Contradictions and Paradoxes

I. The development of the Muslim society in Egypt:

Egypt is one of the leading countries in the Arab Islamic world and the Middle East. Islam in Egypt is the predominant religion comprising more than 90% of the Egyptian population (Scroope, 2017). Almost the entirety of Egypt's Muslims are Sunnis, with a small minority of Shia Muslims, despite the fact that Egypt was the center of the Shia Ismaili caliphate of the Fatimids In the late 10th century (Minority Rights Group International, 2017). Many traces of Fatimid architecture still exist in Cairo today; including Al-Azhar Mosque (Fig. 1), which is now part of a great Islamic University that is considered the center of moderate Sunni teachings, and is the official religious representative of Egypt.

Fig. 1: Al-Azhar Mosque representing the Fatimid Cairo

Egypt serves as an excellent case study for understanding the diverse classifications of Muslim groups present in its society, as it has the largest population of Muslims in the Arab world. Additionally, Egypt has been actively combating Muslim extremist groups till today.

The long western occupation had its impacts on Egyptian society that was highly influenced by westernization during that period. This can be seen in many Egyptian movies showing the life of Egyptian society similar to the European society, especially for the high social class and middle class. Many of the highly educated Egyptians studied in European universities as Egypt sent many students to continue their education abroad. Westernization can be seen among Egyptians in their fashion of clothing, hairstyle, and even in social habits like alcohol drinking that highlighted the scenes representing the Egyptian society under British colonization. The picture in Fig. 2 shows the European style of clothing adopted by the last royal family ruling Egypt. In the picture, the last king of Egypt, King Farouk, wearing the European hat with his sisters all dressed in European fashion.

Source: (Rauf, 2022)

Fig. 2: The Western style of the Egyptian Royal family

Of course, there were always some religious people among Egyptian society, but they were not under the scope of the media. The 1920s witnessed the emergence of the most organized Islamic group of Egypt which is "the Muslim brotherhood".[1] However, the overall image of Egyptian society by that time was still westernized, as introduced by the

---

1 The Muslim Brotherhood was founded in the Egyptian city "Al-Islamailia" in 1928. For more information, see: (The Editors of Encyclopaedia, 2023).

mass media reflecting the social trends of that period.

The influence of Western culture can be seen in many aspects of Egyptian society since the period of European colonization starting with the French occupation (1798-1801) and ending with the British occupation (1882-1954). The French occupation introduced European knowledge and new technology of that time to Egyptian society including the printing press. Thus, through the French printing machines brought by Napoleon Bonaparte, the first newspaper in Egypt with the title "Le Courrier de l'Égypte" was published in French in August 1798 in addition to another weekly French newspaper "La Décade Égyptienne" (Shafik, 1981, pp. 21-22). The picture in Fig. 3 shows issue No. 116 of that first French newspaper published by the French occupation authority in Egypt.

Source: (Wikipedia, 2022)

Fig. 3: First Newspaper published in Egypt

Sooner after the end of French occupation, Egypt started its modernization thanks to the efforts of the new ruler of Egypt, Muhammad Ali, who is also of European origin as he was born in Greece and his family was Albanians, and he served as the governor of Albania under the rule of the Ottoman Empire. Muhammad Ali established his dynasty in Egypt lasting from 1805 till the end of the rule of the last king of his descendants "Farouk" in 1952. Muhammad Ali is considered the Founder of Modern Egypt through his reform project using European modern technology and promoting western education in Egypt (Kia, 2017, p. 87). Thus, we can say that Muhammad Ali strongly continued the Westernization of Egypt which had its first steps in Modern times during the French occupation. The westernization process during the rule of Muhammad Ali included dispatching Egyptian officials and officers to receive training on new technologies and modern education in Europe. Also, he sent missions of Egyptian students to get higher education in Europe, especially to France.[2] Expectedly, those Egyptian officers and students came back to Egypt with the European culture and contributed to the westernization of the Egyptian societies through their interpretation of European culture including literature, arts, and other phases of culture. These westernization efforts continued under the rule of Mohamed Ali's descendants to be one of the features of the rule of Mohamed Ali's family ruled Egypt for a long period that exceeded one century.

During the rule of the Muhammad Ali dynasty, the last European occupation also took place in Egypt through British colonization starting from 1882 and officially ended in 1922 while the departure of the last

---

2   For more details, see: (Silvera, 1980).

British forces was in 1956 (Marsot & Lutfi, 1999, p. 652). The foreign communities grew under this era of the British occupation as foreigners and especially the British and their allies were encouraged to settle in Egypt with many privileges guaranteeing them a life of good quality. Many of the celebrities in Egypt were foreigners or of a foreign origin. Examining the Egyptian cinema since its emergence we can see many of those foreigners settled in Egypt. Famous actors with great contributions to the Egyptian cinema industry like the Jewish Italian Togo Mizrahi (1901-1986), and Stephan Rosti (1891-1964) of an Italian mother and Austrian father are examples of many foreigners settled in Egypt. The Egyptian movies documented the fashion and other social traditions influenced by the West by the end of that period. Despite the Islamic traditions prohibiting alcohol, Egyptians drinking alcohol and the nightlife similar to the Western lifestyle were seen in many scenes of the movies picturing the realistic society of the early years of the twentieth century.

Source: A Screenshot of the Egyptian movie "Al-Azeema" (Selim, 1939).

Fig. 4: Western lifestyle of Egyptian society as shown in the Egyptian Movie "Al-Azeema"

The pictures in Fig. 4 show some common features of the upper class of Egyptian society with their western fashion and western attitude at their parties including drinking alcohol and performing western dances. The pictures are taken for a scene in the Egyptian movie "Al-Azeema" which means "the will" in English, released in 1939. In the same movie we can see the diversity of the fashion style of clothes as the Turkish influence is seen in the tranditional hat called "tarboosh" used by Egyptians, especially in official meetings seen in the first picture in Fig. 8 as three men were wearing the tarboosh and one man was wearing the Egyptian traditional head cover for men known as "e'mma". In the second picture of Fig. 5 the Egyptian traditional clothing style seen in the lady's cloth and the traditional gallabiyah worn by the first man while the other two men mixed their clothes with Turkish, Arab, and Western styles as one is wearing the tarboosh on his western suite and the other is wearing it on his Arab gallabiyah. The traditional Egyptian cloth of gallabiyahs and the head covers are still adopted widely by some Egyptian

Source: A Screenshot of the Egyptian movie "Al-Azeema" (Selim, 1939).

Fig. 5: Diversity of clothes styles seen in the Egyptian Society

ordinary people and mainly in the countryside preserving their culture till today.

Egyptian society continued in the same trend much more similar to European societies than to the traditional Islamic society until the defeat happened in the war of 1967, which was a shock for the whole society. This had its impact on the religious practices of the society, as usually people are closer to God when they face crises, especially when that crisis made the future uncertain. This is how Egyptians who witnessed this defeat tell about it. However, this is believed to be a turning point in the religious attitude of Egyptian society which began to behave more religiously since then. One of the impacts of that military defeat was clear in the economic crisis that Egypt suffered in the 70s, this also may explain the fact the revival of interest in Sufism since the early 1970s.

On the other hand, due to the economic crisis, many Egyptians of the middle class went to work in the Saudi Kingdom and Gulf countries, which also had another impact on the religious attitude and thinking of these people, as they turned back to Egypt influenced by the religious life they had in those countries which formed the Salafi trend since then. Some other Egyptians immigrate to Europe and US and were much influenced in the opposite way.

Accordingly, by the end of the last century, Egyptian society, with its large population, was composed of a diverse array of Muslim groups. Some of them were non-religious and lacked proper Islamic knowledge, primarily residing in impoverished rural communities plagued by poverty and illiteracy. Additionally, some of those non-religious Egyptians were from other social classes including wealthy high-society classes with minimal interest in religion. Furthermore, there existed a broad spectrum of religious individuals, varying in degrees of faith, ranging from extremist to secular Muslims.

II. Classifications of Muslims in the Egyptian Society:

The observer of Egyptians in the streets can notice easily this variety of Muslims, especially in women's customs, as there is a wide range of women's clothes that reflect their religious thinking somehow. The Salafis can be recognized most likely by their dark customs similar to customs of Saudi or Gulf countries, women with ordinary modest Islamic customs may be ordinary Muslims with no affiliation, or maybe Muslim brotherhood members. Also, some women in Egyptian streets would be seen following Turkish fashion or western fashion but in a modest way while keeping their hair covered, besides modern women are beautifully dressed in a fashionable way but keeping their modesty some of them still cover their hair but nicely in a fashionable way that may show some of their hair, some others choose to be modest but without hair cover, and finally another group threw any Islamic custom refusing to admit that it is a part of the religion while others admit that it is part of the religion but they are brave enough to declare that they can't afford it. Besides all these types, of course, there are also some women who are not interested in religion yet though they are Muslims just by name.

Source: (Ahram Press, 2011).

Fig. 6: Diversity of women's styles in Egyptian streets

The picture in Fig. 6 shows a segment of this diversity of Egyptian women in one of Cairo's streets as they stood in a queue to cast their ballots during the Egyptian parliament elections of 2011. This variety also can be seen in each of the social classes in the Egyptian society. The following picture of Figure 7 depicts a group of women who were members of the Egyptian parliament in 2016. This photograph serves as evidence of the diversity presented in Egyptian society, as demonstrated through the varied appearance of these women representing the Egyptian people in the parliament.

Fig. 7: Women in the Egyptian Parliament

In fact, this classification realized by Egyptians themselves has its impact on their opinion judging people by their appearance, especially when religion mixed with politics somehow in the past few years. This was the reason for some Muslim women to change the look of their customs so as to avoid being classified into any specific group. Additionally, some other women seized the opportunity to abandon their head coverings in alignment with the social trends against Islamists. Usually, the term "Islamists" is used to refer to the politically organized Muslims who seek to purge the country of its secular policies including the group of "Muslim brotherhood" which was designated as a terrorist organization in Egypt following the overthrow of their leader from the presidency in 2013.

The following classification for Muslims of Egypt is the one usually adopted by Egyptians themselves as they can recognize it directly through their daily life and can name people around them by these identifications.

Thus, this classification encompasses the various Muslim groups within Egyptian society based on the author's eyewitnesses as an Egyptian who lived inside this society:

a) Muslim Brotherhood   b) Salafi   c) Sufi

d) Quranist   e) non-denominational Muslims

a) Muslim Brotherhood:

The Muslim Brotherhood can be discribed as an Islamist religious, political, and social movement, that was established by its Egyptian leader Hassan al-Banna in Egypt in March 1928. While this group has expanded to other Muslim countries, it has a significant presence in Egypt, where it has long been a powerful political opposition force despite facing government repression in 1948, 1954, and 1965 due to alleged plots of assassination and overthrow.[3]

After the 2011 Revolution in Egypt, the Muslim Brotherhood was legally recognized and in April 2011, it established a political party known as "the Freedom and Justice Party" to participate in the political elections. This included the 2012 presidential election where their candidate, Mohamed Morsi, became Egypt's first democratically elected president. However, a year later, due to widespread protests, Morsi was removed from power. As of 2014, the organization has been designated

---

3   For more details, see: (Hanna, 2016), (Vidino, 2013)

as a terrorist group by various countries such as Russia, Egypt, UAE, and Saudi Arabia which led to severe repression for its members and supporters as well. (BBC, 2013).

Actually, the 2011 revolution was a start of a new era for this group in Egypt, as they start to have a more positive image in the society to the extent that they gained popularity among Egyptian society. But they couldn't make good use of this positive change as they took advantage of this in reaching political power, in a way that negatively again changed their image for the worse until their leader was thrown out of the presidency of Egypt and all other sequences lead to declaring them as a terrorist group. Accordingly, Egyptian society is divided into Egyptians who curse the name of this group, Egyptians who are members of this group, Egyptians who sympathize with this group, and Egyptians who doesn't care about the whole thing due to real ignorance of this issue, or for not being able to give a right judgment or a clear vision. But officially this group is criminated by the Egyptian government.

B) Salafi

The term Salafism is derived from the Arabic word "salaf سلف" which means anscestors or forefathers referring to the early generations of the companions of Islam's prophet Muhammad. Thus, the adjective "Salafi" or "Salafists" refers to those who try to follow the same way adopted by the early Muslim generation in their practices, traditions, and interpretation of the Quran. In the 1300s, a coherent version of Salafism began to develop as a response to inflexible institutions and the alleged corruption of Islamic doctrine and practice. It denounced Sufi activities as well as the strict adherence to particular schools of Islamic law. In the eighteenth century, Salafism flourished throughout the Muslim world, particularly in the Arabian Peninsula, where the successful Salafi movement known as Wahhabism first appeared and continues to this day (Brown, 2011, p. 3). Many Egyptians left their country for employment in Saudi Arabia and other Gulf nations due to the country's ongoing economic problems increasingly since the 1970s. This confirmed the Salafi presence in Egypt by importing Wahabi thought as well.

Before the 2011 revolution in Egypt, Salafis were considered one of the most significant Islamic groups, with more influence than even the Muslim Brotherhood, which is recognized for its well-organized institutions. The Salafis lacked an organized structure and also political objectives as their teachings were not politicized. This explains how the Salafi movement was handled by the Mubarak dictatorship, which tolerated them so long as they did not pose a threat to national security (Brown, 2011, p. 5). Therefore, as long as they didn't discuss politics, Salafi preachers and religious organizations were allowed to exist in peace. However, during the 2011 uprising, Salafis started to get involved in politics and founded Al-Nour, their first political party. After the Muslim Brotherhood's Freedom and Justice Party, this party won the most seats in the Egyptian parliament in the 2011–2012 elections (Inter-Parliamentary Union, 2012).

Although Salafis showed support for the Muslim Brotherhood's leader, Morsi, during his presidency, they also backed the new Egyptian president, Al-Sisi, in his removal of the Muslim Brotherhood's leader from power. Disagreements between Salafis and Muslim Brotherhood was obvious on many occasions ending with each group condemning the other.[4]

The Sufis are another group seriously condemned by Salafis. Especially, Wahabi Muslims strongly criticize the Sufi philosophy and call them a heretical innovative group. This can be seen in the fatwas of Sheikh Abd al Aziz ibn Abdullah Ibn Baz who was the Saudi Grand Mufti in the 1990s (Bin Baz). Thus, the relations between Egyptian Salafi and Sufi witnessed many tensions.

c) Sufi Muslims

Sufism represents the mysticism that can be found in most religions and not only in Islam. Derived from the Arabic word "suf صوف" with the meaning of "wool" referring to the hard clothes those Sufis usually wore, Sufis always showed an ascetic attitude (Ahmed, 2022, p. 31). Most Egyptian Sufis can be distinguished by their meetings held in

---

4 For more details on some incidents, see: (El-Sherif, 2015).

their mosques practicing their special way of worshiping sometimes accompanied by music and some body movements including the famous whirling dance which had its influence on Egyptain traditional folkloric dances called "Tannura" seen in Fig. 8. Especially, the Mawlawiyya order is known of these whirling ritual.

Source: (Kamal, 2011).

Fig. 8: Egyptian Tannura influenced by Sufi whirling

Away from those distinctive Sufi practices, it's hard to distinguish many Sufis in Egyptian society, as they are just ordinary Muslims who worship god in their own way through special gatherings. Thus, it is difficult to give accurate statistics for Sufis as they can also be Sunni or Shi'ite and their classification also intersects with other Muslims. In Egypt, sometimes non-denominational Muslims join Sufi meetings and participate in those Sufi performances and rites based on curiosity, seeking meditation, or even for gaining the benefits of attending those meetings when sharing meals and other charities.[5]

The three main practices identifying Egyptian Sufis are the Sufi meetings called "Dhikr" for praising God, visiting the graves of Sufi saints or shrines of the Prophet's family, and holding "Mawled", the Arabic word for Sufi festivals commemorating birthdays of their late figures. The performances practiced in those events range from reciting Quran and Sufi poems praising God to other performances including dancing, whirling, and even showing supernatural abilities proving the superpower of their fellows in some Sufi orders.

Source: (Mare'i. 2016).

Fig. 9: Sufi supernatural performances

---

5 A documentary produced by BBC News showed the world of Sufis in Egypt through their different rites and the life stories of their fellows. For more details: (BBC News. 2019).

The picture in Fig. 9 shows some of the Sufi performances of their supernaturals in a festival of the al-Rifaaiya order. Officially, there are 78 Sufi orders or sub-groups followed by more than 15 million Egyptians. Among them, al-Rifaaiya order with more than two million fellows is the biggest (Tantawi, 2017)

As previously mentioned in this chapter about the tensions between Salafis and Sufis in Egypt, Unfortunately, Sufis are often targeted by Muslim extremists, particularly those of the Salafi group. This is evidenced by several incidents, such as the 2017 terrorist attack on the al-Rawda mosque in Sinai, Egypt, which resulted in the deaths of 235 Sufis (Walsh & Youssef, 2017).

As for political life, Sufi leaders generally enjoyed good relations with all Egyptian governments especially due to their not being involved in politics as they always represented the soft form of Islam against the hardliners who can be seen in other groups such as Salafis. But, thanks to the 2011 revolution, Sufis were among many Islamic groups who started to find their political parties. Among them, the Tariqa Ar-Rifa'iyyah formed its first political party called "The Voice of Freedom Party", and the Tariqa Al-Azmeyyah founded "The Egyptian Liberation Party". Additionally, Sufi leaders backed the military's removal of the former Islamist President and Muslim Brotherhood representative, Mohammed Morsi, in 2013, in response to widespread protests. They also supported Egyptian President Abdul Fattah al-Sisi in the 2014 presidential election. Those Sufi political parties became secularized and joined other secular political alliances as a result of the constitutional changes that prohibited the formation of political parties based on religion. (Ahmed M. F., 2021). Having positive relationships with liberal Muslims and collaborating politically with them to counter other Islamic parties would have enhanced the relationship between the Sufis and the Egyptian government, and in turn, enhance the good image of Sufis in Egyptian society in general.

The Sufi celebration, Sufi music, and Sufi leaders can be seen frequently on Egyptian official TV channels and other mass media channels supported by the Egyptian government. Many officials, professors, and students of Al-Azhar university, the most prestigious Egyptian Islamic university, are well-known for being Sufis. Among them is Sheikh Ali Gomaa who was the 18th grand Mufti of Egypt (2003-2013) and founder of Egypt's newest Sufi order called Shadhiliyyah Assiddiqiyya (Higazy & Eissa, 2018).

The governmental control over the Sufis can be seen through the role of the Supreme Council of Sufi Orders, which has the authority to give permissions for Sufi activities while ensuring its consistency with Islamic principles. This council consists of ten elected members representing different Sufi tariqas and five appointed members representing Al-Azhar University, the Ministry of Religious Endowments, the Ministry of

Interior, the Ministry of Culture, and Local Administration.[6]

d) Quranists

The Quranists, or the quranic people, are a group of Muslims who reject the authority of hadith and believe only in the Quran, that's why they're called as Quranists "Quraniyoon in Arabic". They showed up in Egypt during the early 20th century. They are considered an innovative group by other Muslim groups, deviating from the path of mainstream Islam. They pose and comment on many issues related to Islam from their viewpoint and reject many fundamental aspects of Islam. They also defend their views and present them as the only right view of Islam. They criticize other Muslim groups for relying on Hadiths that they are not certain in their point of view.

Ahmed Sobhi Mansour is one of the well-known Quranists considered as the founder of this group in Egypt. He is an Islamic researcher who was granted political asylum in the United States in 2002, and He has served as a visiting fellow at the National Endowment for Democracy, and at the Human Rights Program at Harvard Law School. In the US, Mansour has established an international center for the quranic people and continued preaching Quranism as the right form of Islam according to his view. (The International Quranic Center, 2010). He is active

---

6   For more details on the Supreme Council of Sufi Orders in Egypt, see: (Al-Jazeera, 2017).

in publishing his thoughts through the internet and supporting the views of his Quranist group. The Arabic name of the group is "Ahl Al-Quran" which means the people or family of the Quran.

Usually, the Quranists in Egypt cannot be identified unless they reveal their beliefs. Sometimes, they have faced intolerance from both the government and society due to their views being seen as deviant from the accepted Islamic norms. In 2007, four Quranists were arrested on charges of insulting Islam, which elicited criticism from human rights organizations. In November 2009, a Quranist writer was taken into custody at Cairo airport and denied the ability to leave the country. In October 2010, a Quranist blogger was taken into custody in a case of "forced disappearance" and was imprisoned for three months before being freed. (Minority Rights Group International, 2017).

Through my witnesses as an Egyptian, there are roughly two main groups following Quranism. The first is the Quranists who claim the Quran should be the only source for religion, rejecting every other source and Hadith. The second group is the Quranists who do not reject all Hadiths but are very critical of Hadith and reject everything that they believe contradicts the Quran.

Quranists weren't well-known in Egyptian society until they published their opinions in Egyptian mass media and went into debates with famous Sunni men that got the attention of many Egyptian audiences, as the debates were so active and went into serious word fights especially between one of the Quranist who is the Islamic researcher Sayed Alquimni and Sheikh Khaled AlGindi, who is one of Al-Azhar scholars, that was so interesting that made many people share it widely through SNS in 2010.

e) Non–denominational Muslims

There is a substantial number of non-denominational Muslims in Egypt. These are individuals who identify as Muslim but do not align with any specific religious denomination. They persist to name themselves just "Muslim".

Many non-denominational Muslims in Egypt do not pay much attention to the different categorizations of Muslim groups for several reasons. Firstly, some believe that religion is a personal relationship between an individual and God and that it is not necessary to interfere with others' beliefs. They see the diversity of opinions among different sects as acceptable and may study their beliefs for knowledge purposes only, not to follow them.

Secondly, some may not care much about religion itself and identify as Muslim simply because it was passed down from their parents. The third reason would be that some others may not have had the opportunity to study their religion deeply due to work, study, or other life pursuits, and therefore practice Islam based on what they learned in their childhood. They may not be aware of the differences between Muslim sects and may not feel the need to learn more at the time, but may decide to do so in the future if they have the opportunity.

Another reason that some Muslim Egyptians may have no religious affiliation to any sect could be ignorance and poverty. There is still a significant portion of Egyptians who suffer from illiteracy, particularly in rural areas. For these individuals, studying religion is an unattainable luxury as they cannot even read a book. They simply identify as Muslims because they were born into the religion.

The non-denominational Muslim population in Egypt encompasses individuals at opposite ends of the spectrum, both illiterate and culturally knowledgeable. Some within this group seek to deepen their understanding of Islam through self-study using books or media, or by attending regular courses on the Quran and Islamic studies. However, others have limited access to religious resources and are unable to read.

Additionally, the Egyptian non-denominational Muslims include modern liberal Muslims, who can be considered culturally knowledgeable or intellectuals. However, some liberal Muslims may have limited knowledge of Islam and are more focused on upholding principles of freedom and liberation. They often believe that much of the Muslim world blindly follows backward teachings without proper understanding. In turn, those liberal Muslims are frequently criticized by conservative Muslims for their lack of proper Islamic understanding.

III. The Cultural diversity of Egyptian society:

We can see that Egypt has a cultural diversity that can be seen in many different cultures including ancient Egyptian, Arab, Coptic, western, Turkish, and other cultures that mixed and exchanged throughout Egypt's history with a long period of foreign rulers and foreign settlers as well. Multiculturalism can be examined through many different cultural groups living in Egypt including Berbers, Nubians, Copts, Bedouins, and other minorities.

This cultural diversity and the different historical roots of those groups resulted in different traditions and customs among the Muslim community in Egypt. Some Muslim families are mixed with other religious groups like Jews or Christians as Islam allows men to marry women of these religions. Thus, those families mix both cultures. Thus, some of the traditions and customs followed by many Egyptians actually violate Islamic traditions. An example would be using some ancient Egyptian symbols and amulets to bring good luck and ward off envy. The picture in Fig. 10 shows some of those amulets of the ancient Egyptian heritage that are still fashionable at present in Egypt.

The ancient Egyptian scarab amulet
Source: (Benzie, 2005)

The hieroglyph sign of
Ankh which refers to life.
Source: (The Metropolitan Museum of Art.)

Fig. 10: Ancient Egyptian amulets

Source: (Waheesh, 2017).

Fig. 11: The Nubian bracelet

Some ethnic groups in Egypt preserve their traditions and customs which sometimes also include practices contrary to Islam. The picture in Fig. 11 shows the Nubian bracelet made of red threads with a white shell, which is still traditionally worn by the Nubian groom at his wedding to protect him from evil eyes.

In brief, we can say that many aspects of cultural diversity can be seen in Egyptian Muslim society. There are distinctive cultures in each Egyptian region. Thus, there are differences between Egyptians in the Sinai region who are Bedouins, compared to other Egyptians in South

Egypt, or Delta region, or the coast of the Mediterranean.

Another cultural dimension that has a deep influence on Egypt is the long foreign rule in Egypt throughout history. Beginning with Greeks, and followed by Romans, Foreigners ruling Egypt persistently continued until the modern era, as the last king of Egypt, King Farouk, was also a foreigner with Albanian roots. For centuries Egyptians were ruled by foreigners and lived together with many different races. The cultures of those foreigners mixed and interacted with Egyptian culture resulting in a unique culture. The language of Egyptians reflects this mixture, as Egyptian Arabic has still words of many languages starting with words from the Egyptian language of Ancient times to the Turkish, French, and English languages of modern times.

Through a long time of foreign occupation, many foreigners settled in Egypt and mixed with Egyptians. At present, those old foreign communities still have their marks on Egyptian society. So, we can trace Greeks, Turks, Italians, Armenians, and other foreigners still having their own communities in Egypt. In addition to many Egyptians with foreign origins. Personally, my husband's grandfathers are Turkish, and many of my Egyptian friends have foreign ancestors.

The impact of foreign origins on Egyptian customs and traditions can be easily observed, particularly in the westernization of Egyptian wedding ceremonies. Modern Egyptian weddings are mainly modeled after Western weddings, with wedding venues often being held in Western-style hotels, brides wearing white dresses, grooms donning Western-style suits, the tradition of throwing the bouquet, and other similar practices.

The picture in Fig. 12 proves this Western influence seen in the western clothes of the Egyptian bride and bridegroom at their wedding in Cairo attended by Egyptian President Nasser in 1963.

Source: (Alrikabi, 2012).

Fig. 12: Egypt's President Nasser attending a wedding in Cairo in 1963

On the other hand, we have also many Egyptians who immigrated to other countries and finally returned to settle with their families again in Egypt while bringing the cultures of other countries. In 2019, Egypt had the largest number of people living abroad according to the World Migration report of the UN for 2020. The emigration trend increased since it was recognized as a constitutional right according to the 1971 Constitution. The estimated number of Egyptian living abroad exceeded

9.5 million Egyptians since 2017 as declared by the Egyptian Central Agency for Public Mobilization and Statistics. Among those Egyptians abroad about 70% live in Arab countries (Mostly Saudi Arabia and other Gulf countries), and the rest of Egyptian abroad live mostly in North America (the United States and Canada), Europe, and Australia. Those Egyptians also contribute to multiculturalism through the foreign cultures they gain in their living abroad and thus transmitting those cultures to Egyptian society through their visits or contact with families and friends in Egypt. In this context, we can refer to the previously mentioned influence of Wahabism in the emergence of the Salafi movement in Egypt, as this was brought by Egyptians who lived in Saudi Arabia. Similarly, other Egyptians who immigrated to Europe or the US brought more westernization to Egyptian society with many traditions violating Islam, especially in the western appearance for women liberated from the Islamic strict for women's clothes.

Another dimension deeply affects the diversity of Egyptian society is education. Examining the education institutions in Egypt, we can see a clear diversity mixed with multiculturalism through the foreign educational institutions presented different foreign educational systems found in all levels of education starting with kindergartens to schools and universities. American, British, French, German, and recently Japanese and Korean universities are a few examples of those foreign institutions providing an official system of education following their culture.

Accordingly, Egyptian students learn and gain those foreign cultures through those educational institutions.

In turn, Egyptian universities were leading institutions in the region and that also attracted students from other countries to come to Egypt to get their education in Egyptian universities like Cairo university, and Al-Azhar university, which is considered the most prestigious university of Sunni Islamic education attracting yearly about 30,000 students from over 100 countries all over the world. Those Foreign students also exert their influence on Egyptian society through their extended stay during their studies, and some even marry Egyptians and choose to settle in Egypt.

IV. Paradoxes and contradictions among Egyptian Muslims

The rich cultural diversity in Egypt leads to many paradoxes and contradictions. This chapter has explored the different classifications present in Egyptian Muslim society. One such paradox is the presence of religious diversity within a majority Sunni Muslim population. Despite the majority of Egyptians being Sunni, they are divided into different subsects, with some disputes even occurring between them.

Another paradox is the coexistence of religious conservatism and secularism, the harmonious relations between the Sufis and the Egyptian government, alongside their rivalry with Salafi groups who also maintain relatively good ties with the government. Yet,, the relationship between the Sufis and Salafis with the Muslim Brotherhood is tense and marked by their rejection of the Brotherhood and agreement with the government's classification of them as a terrorist group.

It is also notable that the norms of these Islamic groups change to match the political context. For example, Sufis, who were once known for their avoidance of political participation, have established political parties and become involved in the political process. Similarly, Salafi groups made use of the 2011 revolution to participate in political life by creating their own political parties.

Another contradiction can be seen in the relationship between Sufis, liberals, and Islamists. In the first parliamentary elections after the 2011 revolution, Sufis and liberals found common ground and worked together against the Islamists. This showed that even though the Sufis are considered a relatively conservative religious group, they chose to align with liberals instead of with Islamists.

In conclusion, it is essential to understand that the composition of the Egyptian Muslim society, although appearing consistent with its majority belonging to the same Islamic sect, is much more complex and involves a diverse range of contradictions and paradoxes. This misleading consistency in the religious composition of the society can give an impression of a lack of pluralism, but the reality is much different.

Egyptian society has been subject to various foreign influences, including long periods of foreign occupation, which has led to changes in its Islamic norms and greater westernization of its traditions. The presence of different ethnic groups within Egyptian society has also contributed to the preservation of their unique traditions and customs, sometimes conflicting with traditional Islamic norms.

Moreover, the coexistence of religious conservatism and secularism, the existence of religious diversity within a majority Muslim population, and the changes in the norms of various Islamic groups based on political context are just a few examples of the contradictions and paradoxes that exist within Egyptian Muslim society. Furthermore, several factors contribute to the intensification of these contradictions and paradoxes within the Egyptian Muslim society. One of the most prominent factors is the huge disparity between the wealthy and the poor, which often leads to social and economic inequalities. Additionally, poverty and illiteracy play a significant role in deepening these contradictions, as individuals with limited resources and education may not have the necessary tools and understanding to navigate the complexities of religious and cultural diversity within their society. These factors, along with the various influences from both foreign and domestic sources, all work together to create a rich and diverse but also complex society that requires further study and research to fully comprehend.

■ References

Ahmed, M. F. (2021, Sep. 9). *Sufism in Egypt.* Retrieved from Institute for Mediterranean Studies: http://ims.or.kr/ims/essay/23

Ahmed, M. F. (2022). Tracking the Sufi presence in Jerusalem. *Annals of Korean Association of the Islamic Studies (KAIS), 32*(3), 29-56.

Ahram Press. (2011, Nov. 28). *New campaign aims to provide marginalised women with national IDs.* Retrieved from Ahram online: https://english.ahram.org.eg/ NewsContent/1/64/37451/Egypt/Politics-/New-campaign-aims-to-provide-marginalised-women-wi.aspx

Al-Jazeera. (2017, Dec. 4). *The Supreme Council of Sufi Orders in Egypt "المجلس الأعلى للطرق الصوفية بمصر".* Retrieved from Al-Jazeera: https://www.aljazeera. net/encyclopedia/2017/12/4/المجلس-الأعلى-للطرق-الصوفية-بمصر

Alrikabi, A. (2012, Dec. 10). *Fouad Al-Rikabi's wedding ceremony-Cairo 1963, in the presence of Gamal Abdel Nasser.* Retrieved from commons.wikimedia: https://commons.wikimedia.org/wiki/File:Fouad_Alrikabi_-_Wedding_-_ Cairo_1963.jpg

Anadolu Agency. (2016, Jan. 10). *Women parliamentarians attend an inaugural parliament session in Cairo.* Retrieved from The Cairo Review: https://www. thecairoreview.com/essays/are-egyptian-women-empowered/

Angelpeream. (2011, Jan. 31). *Islam branches and schools.* Retrieved from Wikipedia: https://ko.wikipedia.org/wiki/%EC%9D%B4%EC%8A%AC%EB%9E%8 C%EA%B5%90#/media/%ED%8C%8C%EC%9D%BC:Islam_branches_ and_schools.svg

Ayad, M. (2018, June 11). *Al-Azhar Mosque.* Retrieved from wikimedia: https:// commons.wikimedia.org/wiki/File:جامع_الازهر.jpg

BBC. (2013, Dec. 25). *Egypt's Muslim Brotherhood declared 'terrorist group.* Retrieved from BBC NEWS: https://www.bbc.com/news/world-middle-east-25515932

BBC News. (2019, Nov. 12). *Sufi Ecstasy: a journey through spiritual Egypt.* Retrieved from BBC World Service: https://www.youtube.com/watch?v=UqKXX9PcV3I&t=39s

Benzie, R. (2005, Oct. 18). *Scarab amulet, 550 BC.* Retrieved from Wikipedia: https://ar.wikipedia.org/wiki/جعران_فرعوني#/media/ملف:Scarab550bc.jpg

Bin Baz, A. (n.d.). The reality of Sufism. *Bin Baz Official website*, pp. https://binbaz.org.sa/fatwas/3237/حقيقة-منهج-الصوفية

Brown, J. (2011, Dec.). Salafis and Sufis in Egypt. *The Carnegie Papers*, 1-26.

DinajGao. (2010, Feb 1). *Map of predominantly Sunni or Shi'a regions in the world.* Retrieved from Wikimedia: https://commons.wikimedia.org/wiki/File:Sunni-Shi%27a_map.png

El-Sherif, A. (2015, April 29). Egypt's Salafists at a Crossroads. *Political Islam in Egypt*, pp. 1-38.

Hanna, M. W. (2016). *The Muslim Brotherhood in Egypt: A Guide to the World's Most Powerful Islamist Movement.* New York: Oxford University Press.

Higazy, S., & Eissa, A.-W. (2018, July 21). *The Shadhiliyah Assiddiqiya Siddiqiyah is the 78th order of Sufism in Egypt and the 7th of Al-Azhar* ("الصيديقية الشاذلية" الطريقة الـ78 للصوفية في مصر والـ7 "الأزهرية"). Retrieved from Elwatan News: https://www.elwatannews.com/news/details/3539654

Hunter, M. T. (2014, June 29). Islam percent population in each nation World Map Muslim data by Pew Research. *Wikimedia Commons.*

Inter-Parliamentary Union. (2012, Jan. 11). *Egypt People's Assemply Election in 2011.* Retrieved from http://archive.ipu.org/parline-e/reports/arc/2097_11.htm

Kamal, M. (2011, Oct. 26). *Tannura Image from Egypt.* Retrieved from Wikimedia Commons: https://upload.wikimedia.org/wikipedia/commons/6/رقصة_التنورة_التراثية_-_مصر/6f.jpg

Khan, A. (2009). Protection of Languages and Self-Expressions under Islamic Law. *Journal of Transnational Law & Policy, 19*(1), 61-122.

Kia, M. (2017). *The Ottoman Empire: A Historical Encyclopedia [2 volumes].* Santa Barbara CA : ABC-CLIO.

Lahrouchi, M. (2018). The Amazigh influence on Moroccan Arabic: Phonological and morphological borrowing. *International Journal of Arabic Linguistics, 4*(1), 39-58.

Mare'i, A. (2016, July 25). *al-Rifaaiya order celebrations in Luxor.* Retrieved from youm7: https://www.youm7.com/story/2016/7/25/بالفيديو-والصور-مواقع-التواصل-الاجتماعى-رصد-قاليد-الصوفية-فى-الموالد/2815708

Marsot, A.-S., & Lutfi, A. (1999). The British Occupation of Egypt from 1882. In A. Porter, & W. R. Louis, *The Oxford History of the British Empire: Volume III: The Nineteenth Century* (pp. 651-664). Oxford: Oxford Academic. doi:https://doi.org/10.1093/acprof:oso/9780198205654.003.0028

Minority Rights Group International. (2017, Oct.). *World Directory of Minorities and Indigenous Peoples - Egypt : Quranists of Egypt,.* Retrieved from Refworld-UNHCR: https://www.refworld.org/docid/5a0582207.html

Minority Rights Group International. (2017, Oct.). *World Directory of Minorities and Indigenous Peoples - Egypt : Shi'a of Egypt.* Retrieved from UNCHCR: https://www.refworld.org/docid/5a059a067.html

Netchev, S. (2021, June 8). *Islamic Conquests between the 7th-9th Centuries.* Retrieved from World History Encyclopedia: https://www.worldhistory.org/image/14212/islamic-conquests-in-the-7th-9th-centuries/

Rauf, F. (2022, May 18). *King Farouq and his sisters.* Retrieved from Wikipedia: https://it.wikipedia.org/wiki/Faiza_Rauf

Scroope, C. (2017). *Egyptian Culture.* Retrieved from Cultural Atlas: https://culturalatlas.sbs.com.au/egyptian-culture/egyptian-culture-religion

Selim, K. (Director). (1939). *Al-Azeema (The Will)* [Motion Picture]. Retrieved from https://www.dailymotion.com/video/x8ew3by

Shafik, F. F. (1981). *The Press and Politics of Modern Egypt: 1798-1970. A Comparative Analysis of Causal Relationships.* New York: New York University ProQuest Dissertations Publishing.

Silvera, A. (1980). The First Egyptian Student Mission to France under Muhammad Ali. *Middle Eastern Studies, 16*(2), 1-22.

Tantawi, G. (2017, Nov. 28). *Who are Egypt's Sufi Muslims?* Retrieved from BBC Monitoring: https://www.bbc.com/news/world-middle-east-42154626

Tas, L. (2014). *Legal Pluralism in Action: Dispute Resolution and the Kurdish Peace Committee.* New York: Routledge.

The Editors of Encyclopaedia. (2023, Jan. 20). *Muslim Brotherhood.* Retrieved from Encyclopedia Britannica: https://www.britannica.com/topic/Muslim-Brotherhood

The Egyptian Dar Al-Ifta. (n.d.). *What is the correct way to burry the dead and the correct shape of graves?* Retrieved from Dar Al-Ifta Al-Missriyyah: https://www.dar-alifta.org/Foreign/ViewFatwa.aspx?ID=6964

The International Quranic Center. (2010, January 31). *IQC Mission Statement.* Retrieved from Ahl-alquran: https://www.ahl-alquran.com/English/aboutus.php

The Metropolitan Museum of Art. (n.d.). *Ceremonial Implement in the Shape of an Ankh.* Retrieved from Metmuseum: https://www.metmuseum.org/art/collection/search/544840

Vidino, L. (2013). *Inside the Muslim Brotherhood: Religion, Identity, and Politics.* New York: Columbia University Press.

Waheesh, M. (2017, June 9). *Nubian beliefs: red threads and a white shell to protect the groom (معتقدات نوبية خيوط حمراء وقوقعة بيضاء لحماية العريس).* Retrieved from Akhbar

Elyom: https://akhbarelyom.com/news/newdetails/2508707/1/معتقدات-نوبية-
خيوط-حمراء-وقوقعة-بيضاء-لح

Walsh, D., & Youssef, N. (2017, Nov. 24). *Militants Kill 305 at Sufi Mosque in Egypt's Deadliest Terrorist Attack.* Retrieved from The New York Times: https://www.nytimes.com/2017/11/24/world/middleeast/mosque-attack-egypt.html

Wikipedia. (2022, Aug. 3). *le Courrier d'Egypte number 116.* Retrieved from Wikipedia: https://en.wikipedia.org/wiki/Courrier_de_l%27%C3%89gypte#/media/File:Courier_egypte_116.jpg

World Population Review. (2022). *Muslim Population by Country 2022.* Retrieved from World Population Review: https://worldpopulationreview.com/country-rankings/muslim-population-by-country

Chapter 4

Tribal Plurality among Muslims in Libya

I. An overview on the Libyan Society:

Libya, located in North Africa, is one of the Arab Muslim countries with a strategic location on the Mediterranean coast, facing Italy and Greece (See the map in Fig. 1). This proximity has made it a major gateway for immigrants seeking to reach Europe. In turn, this location invited Italian colonization to settle in Libya for over three decades. Libyans used to live as nomadic Bedouins in the desert covering the Libyan lands. However, the discovery of oil in the 1950s led to a significant transformation of Libya's economy, elevating it to one of the highest-income countries in Africa. The recent civil war, which involved interventions from NATO and other countries sheds light on the importance of Libya in the region.[1]

Source: (PAT Portable Atlas)

Fig. 1: The map of Libya

The modern Libyan state started forming as a part of the Ottoman Empire in the mid of the sixteenth century. In 1911, Italy conquered Libya with a colonial rule that lasted until World War II. Libya obtained its independence under the Sanusi monarchy supported by the United Nations in 1951. Under the rule of that Libyan monarchy established in eastern Cyrenaica in the late 1800s, Libya experienced hardships in

---

1　For more details, see: (Brown, Buru, Barbour, Cordell, & Fowler, 2023).

turning into a modern nation. Despite the oil industry starting in the 1960s and providing financial relief for the government, the growing power concentration within the monarchy led to a military coup led by Gaddafi in 1969 starting a new era of Libyan history under the rule of Gadhafi. After ruling for more than four decades, Gaddafi was eventually overthrown in 2011 following a civil war. Currently, Libya still faces insecurity and unsettlement after the civil war restarted in 2014, highlighting the relations between the various tribes in Libyan society.[2] This was a summary of Libya's modern history, which includes its experiences of prolonged Ottoman rule followed by Italian colonization before finally achieving independence in the mid-twentieth century. Unfortunately, Libyan society still suffers unsettlement since the 2011's revolution.

According to the Worldometer elaboration based on the latest UN data, the number of the Libyan population was recorded as 7,114,497 on 10 February 2023 (Worldometers, 2023). The Libyan society consists mainly of Arabs or mixed Amazigh-Arabs in addition to minorities of Amazigh, and other ethnicities of African origins. About 97% of the Libyan population consists of Arabs and Amazigh while the rest 3% are of other minorities. The Amazigh of Libya who were the indigenous people of North Africa themselves consist of different ethnic groups.

---

2 For more details about Libyan history, see: (Mundy, 2021).

They mostly live in the west of Libya close to the Algerian border. The Amazigh people of Libya make up around 16% of the population. They live in various parts of the country while they are not geographically connected. In the west, they live near the Mediterranean coast, and in the southeast near the border with Egypt. Tripoli has a significant Amazigh community (IWGIA, 2022). The south is traditionally inhabited by the Tuareg people who are nomadic, pastoralist tribes spread across Libya and other neighboring countries like Niger, Mali, and Algeria. They includes also recent immigrants from Niger and Mali who settled in Libya since the 1970s. The Toubou is another minority of African origin living in the South of Libya. They are mainly centered in the Tibesti Mountains. They suffered persecution under the rule of Gaddafi which led to their participation in the Libyan revolution against him in 2011. Additionally, there are some Arabs with West African origins inhabiting the southern oases (MRG, 2018).

As for the religion, Sunni Islam is the official and nationally dominant sect in Libya. According to the 2021 Report on International Religious Freedom of the US Department of State, the population of Libya is primarily composed of Sunni Muslims, who make up between 90 and 95 percent. Another Muslim sect found among the Libyan population is only a small group of Ibadi Muslims with about 4.5 to 6 percent of the population while some foreigners living in Libya belong to the Ahmadi Muslim sect. There are also Amazigh ethnic minority members who are

Ibadi Muslims. Some Libyan Muslims follow Sufism. The rest of the population includes small religious minorities of Christians, Hindus, Baha'is, and Buddhists, mostly composed of foreigners. In this context, it is worth mentioning that immigrants in Libya make up over 12% of the total Libyan population. Almost all non-Muslim residents are foreigners. The number of Christians in the country is estimated to be 34,600, according to the 2022 World Watch List Country Profile by Open Doors USA. Out of these, around 150 to 180 are Libyan nationals who converted from Islam, while the rest are migrant workers. The foreign Christian communities mostly consist of sub-Saharan African migrants and Filipino workers, with smaller numbers of Egyptian migrants and a few other foreign residents of European nationalities (Office of International Religious Freedom, 2022, p. 2). Thus, we can see that the diversity can't be seen in the religious or ethnic scene of Libyan society as it mostly consists of one Muslim sect with mainly one ethnic group of Arabs.

On the other hand, although the ethnicity of the Libyan people is mainly Arab it includes a huge tribal division estimated with approximately 140 different tribes including many tribes with branches stretching over international borders into neighboring counties of Tunisia, Egypt, and Chad. In eastern Libya, the most powerful tribes are the nine Saadi tribes that are descended from the Banu Sulaym. The Bara'sa tribe is the most influential among them, with a significant presence in Benghazi and Derna. Gadhafi's second wife was also a member of the Bara'sa tribe.

Other prominent tribes in the area include the Awaqir, Magharba, Abid, Urfa, Ubaidat, Hasa, Fawaid, and Dursa. The Awaqir tribe played a key role in opposing colonialism and struggling against the Ottoman and Italian forces, and also had members in senior positions within Gadhafi's regime. The Misrata tribe, with significant influence in Benghazi and Derna, was largely opposed to Gadhafi's rule. Some tribes have members across Libya, such as the Firjan tribe with members in Ajdabiya, Sirte, Zliten, and Tripoli, and a branch in Tunisia. The Zuwayya, Warfalla, Magarha, and Maslata tribes dominate Fezzan but also have importance in the hinterland of Tripoli. Most people in Tripoli are affiliated with the

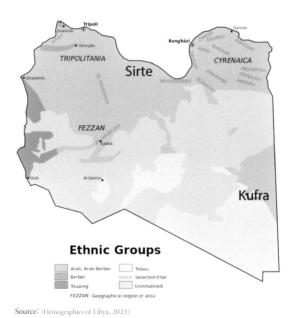

Source: (Demographics of Libya, 2023)

Fig. 2: The ethnic and tribal map of Libya

Misrata tribe, with prominent clans such as Muntasir, Suni, Qadi, and al-Bashti. There are also mixed Arab-Amazigh tribes known as Marabtin, including the Fawakhir, Mnifa, and Qatan. Two of these tribes, the Awlad Nuh and the Awlad al-Shaykh, act more independently and serve as traditional mediators in disputes (Fanack Foundation, 2020).

The map in Fig. 2 shows the main ethnic and tribal distribution in Libya which highlights the tribal plurality and diversity distinguishing the Libyan society. According to the map, we can divide Libya into 5 main regions of Tripolitan in the northwest, Cyrenican in the east, Sirte in the middle of the northern part, Fezzan in the southwest, and Kufra in the southeast. The Arab tribes and Arab-Berber tribes cover the largest part of the North and the middle of the country while some of them live also in some parts of the Kufra in the southeast. Some examples of the places of those Arab tribes can be seen on the map such as Siaan (or Si'an) of Tripolitania, El-Hasawna of Fezzan, Al-Magharba of Sirte, and Bara'sa of Cyrenaica. The Berber tribes can be seen in some small parts of the northwestern parts of Tripolitania. The Touareg tribes live in the western boundaries close while the Tebu (or Toubou) tribes live in the south and southeastern regions.

As the number of Libyan tribes is too many to be listed on this map, we can mention here more of the main tribes in each region. In Tripolitan, there are the settled tribes of Misurata Karagula, Misurata Ahali, Geryan, Zwara Berber, Zawia, Misalata, Khumus, and Bedouin tribes of Warfalla, Tarhona, Al-Zintan, Al-Rijban, and Awlad Suleiman. In Cyrenaican Bedouin tribes: Al-Awagir, Al-Abaydat, Drasa, Al-Bara'sa, Al-Fawakhir, Al-Zuwayya, and Al-Majabra. In Sirte, the main Bedouin tribes include Awlad Suleiman, Qadhadhfa, Al-Magarha, Al-Magharba, Al-Riyyah, Al-Haraba, Al-Zuwaid, and Al-Guwaid. In Fezzan, main tribes are Awlad Suleiman, Hutman, Hassawna, Toubou, and Tuareg. Finally, in Kufra, the main tribes are Al-Zuwayya and Toubou. Berber tribes include Adyrmachidae, Auschisae, Es'bet, Temeh'u, Teh'nu, Rebu, Kehek, KeyKesh, Imukehek, Meshwesh, Macetae, Macatutae, Nasamones, Nitriotae, and Tautamaei (Kawalya-Tendo, 2020, p. 74).

The plurality of the tribal structure, with over a hundred tribes in Libya, is one of the main characteristics distinguishing the Libyan society from other North African Societies. The concept of diversity also can be emphasized by seeing the different origins and traditions of those tribes. In the following section of this chapter, we will explore the roots of those tribes and the relationships between them to highlight this diversity.

II. The historical roots of tribalism in Libya:

Let's first define the concept of "Tribalism". The term itself indicates its connection with the tribes as the basic unit in some societies. Thus, we can simply define Tribalism as a social system based on tribes. The key aspect of tribes is that they share common elements, such as traditions and customs, and may also include a common ethnic origin (Herráez, 2023, p. 4). Exploring tribalism in Libyan society, we can see that Tribalism has a strong historical presence in Libyan society, where tribal affiliations often play a dominant role in the political landscape. The tribal alliances always contributed to the political sphere in Libya which was evident in the emergence of the Senusi monarch under Ottoman rule, its role in resisting the Italian colonization, and continued its role under Ghaddafi's rule showing its negative impact on all the civil wars risen after the 2011 revolution.

The historical roots of tribalism in Libya extend deeply starting with the name of this country. "Libya", the name itself is based on one of the Ancient Berber tribes called "Libu". Since the Arab conquest of Libya, the continuous migration of Arab tribes and families to this country over time has created complexities in the development of Libyan society and has resulted in the formation of new tribes through marriages, trade, and location. This has led to distinctions and hierarchy among the tribes. On the other hand, Libyans have maintained strong connections with Tunisia and Egypt through solidarity, marriages, economics, migration, and tribally-based affiliations that cross the borders of the Libyan state. This is why the 2011 events in Libya had significant repercussions. (Ben Lamma, 2017, pp. 4-5).

The Libyan case presents an excellent opportunity for studying the impact of tribalism as a prominent social organization with substantial influence in various aspects of society. The functions of the tribe are apparent in many social domains, including conflict resolution. In such instances, the tribe often serves as a local mediator and arbitrator, particularly in cases involving property disputes, family matters such as marriage, inheritance, and complaints, as well as crimes such as rape and murder. Although tribal intervention may contribute to the efficiency of the formal justice system, it is not viewed as a replacement for it. The benefits of utilizing tribal justice include its accessibility, swiftness, transparency, and lower levels of corruption compared to the formal system. However, it is crucial to note that tribal justice does not represent a parallel system to the formal justice system of the state. Tribal arbitration and mediation are founded on the community's collective beliefs and are upheld through social pressure, making the tribal mediator or leader more capable of ensuring the implementation of tribal decisions (Ben Lamma, 2017, pp. 6-7).

Examining the history of Libya since the Arab conquest, we can see a connection between its landscape and the nomadic origins of the Arab people. Unlike other North African territories conquered by Arabs, such as Egypt and Tunisia, the preservation of a nomadic lifestyle was more applicable in Libya due to its large desert and limited resources available to its relatively smaller population. Thus, it is understandable that for much of Libya's history, the central government was weak or even absent while the tribes controlled most of the local governance. This was more evident after the fall of Gaddafi regime when the tribal conflicts over political power fueled the civil war.

The Arab migrations since the Arab conquest contributed to the Arabization of Libya while emphasizing the Arab social culture, which gradually dominated the tribal culture of the native ethnic groups in Libya such as the Amazigh, Tuareg, and Tebu. In some regions, clans claiming pure bloodline to the Prophet and his companions dominated other tribes through birthright or conquest, while in others, Arab Bedouin clans formed alliances with non-Arab clans for protection. The bonding process in rural areas led to the formation of tribes, and in urban areas, it resulted in the creation of city-states as trading families and residents banded together to protect their city's interests against the government. This style of the city-state and anti-government politics still prevails today (Cole & Mangan, 2016, p. 5).

The evolution of state building in Libya has been characterized by a recurring pattern of formation and collapse. During the Italian colonial rule, the Ottoman bureaucracy that existed in Libya was dismantled, and the Libyan people were not integrated into the new administrative systems established by the Italians. The Tripolitanian Republic, established after World War I under the leadership of Sulayman al-Baruni[3] failed to gain international recognition and dissolved in 1923.

---

3   He was a prominent Libyan figure of Berber origin. In 1916, he was appointed by the Ottomans as the governor of Tripolitania. For more details on his life, see: (Cresti, 2020).

The independence of Libya in 1951 led to the establishment of the United Kingdom of Libya, but this was followed by the erosion of state institutions during Gadhafi's rule, who dismantled the bureaucratic structures and suppressed civil society organizations and political parties (El-Taraboulsi, 2020, p. 79). In this context, seeing the continuity of the strong tribal affiliations in Libya, we can find links between the strength of tribalism and the weakness of the central government. As expected, the tribal dynamics would have complicated the efforts to establish a functioning central government, as the various tribes compete for power and resources. We can also see that throughout Libyan history, tribalism has often been used by leaders to mobilize support, which resulted in fragmented loyalties hindering the development of a unified national identity.

The role of tribalism is evident in the formation of the Libyan modern state from the beginning, as seen in the establishment of the Tripolitanian Republic in 1918, which was the first republic in the Arab world. The republic was established at a meeting of the tribal leaders of the region. Unlike the eastern region of Libya, which supported the leadership of the Sanusiyah clan, the western region lacked a clear consensus on leadership. Therefore, a Council of Four was established as the ruling body, composed of leaders from different tribes. The republic was headquartered in Aziziyah and had an advisory group of 24 members to represent parties of different regions (El-Taraboulsi, 2020, pp. 46–47). Thus, the influence of the tribal leaders was evident seeing their role in the politics of Libya establishing this first Libyan republic. There were efforts for unifying the Libyan tribes and promoting the national identity can be seen in the past through the Sanusi movement,[4] which contributed to the development of modern Libyan tribalism, and also more recently under the Gaddafirule as the tribal leaders were marginalized, and the government attempted to break the power of tribes by promoting a centralized state structure. This led to a decline in the influence of tribes in Libyan society, but they regained their importance in the aftermath of the 2011 revolution.[5]

Briefly, tracing the historical roots of tribalism in Libya as introduced in this section of the book, we can see that those tribal roots are closely tied to the country's political, social, and economic developments as tribes have played a crucial role in shaping the modern Libyan state.

---

4 The founder of the Sanusi Sufi order was Sayyid Muhammad bin Ali al-Sanusi, who was born in Algeria. He settled in Cyrenaica and by the 1840s he preached his Sufi order in other regions of Libya. In 1843, he established the first lodge for breaching the Sanusi order which extended to other neighboring countries with the continuous efforts of his successors. For more details, see: (Raza. 2012, pp. 93–95).

5 For more details about the tribal situation during and after the Gaddafiera, see: (Basu. 2011).

III. Impacts of the tribal plurality on the political landscape

Upon examining the historical roots of tribalism in Libya, it becomes evident that the influence of tribal affiliation has been a prominent feature of Libya's political landscape both prior to and following the 2011 revolution. Throughout Libya's history, tribal identity has served as a channel for obtaining rights and access to state institutions. Despite the country being home to 140 distinct tribes, a mere 30 of them hold influential power (Ali, 2014, p. 46).

In the following part of this chapter, we can explore the political role of those influential Libyan tribes while distinguishing between them based on their geographical location as some of them are situated in the western region, while others are located in the eastern part of the country. The following are some examples of those influential tribes in Libya:

a) **Warfalla**, the largest tribe in Libya with about one million persons representing a sixth of the Libyan population. In 1993, the tribe staged a coup against Gadhafi, calling for greater representation in government, with the backing of the Magarha tribe. They are opposing the Islamists in their rise in Libya (Apps, 2011).

b) **Magarha**, the second largest tribe in Libya. It has contributed to the political process in Libya with a central role through its members including influential leaders who supported Gaddafi during certain periods of his rule, while at other times they also joined the uprisings against him. This tribe also opposes the Islamists (Apps, 2011).

c) Tarhouna, it encompasses a significant number of sub-tribes, totaling about sixty which comprises roughly one-third of Tripoli's population. In April 2020, the tribal leaders of Tarhouna announced their support for the military commander Khalifa Haftar to be one of his strongholds in his fight against the internationally recognized Government of National Accord (GNA). Later on, in June 2020, mass graves were found in the town of Tarhouna showing their sufferance under the control of the Kaniyat militia, which allied with Khalifa Haftar during his 2019 attack on the Government of National Accord (Harchaoui, 2020).

d) Misrata, the most influential tribe in eastern Libya, which has a strong presence in Benghazi and Darneh. It was opposing Gaddafi while supporting Islamists which is evident in the formation of the "Libya Dawn" coalition between the Islamist and Misratan militias in 2014. The Misurata region has experienced a division over the past 50 years, with some people abandoning traditional tribal pursuits to live in urban centers. Among the more notable tribes and families that have done so are the el-Mahjoub clan, Zamoura family, Kawafi tribe, Dababisa tribe, Zawaiya tribe, al-Sawalih tribe, and al-Jarsha tribe (Hatitah, 2011). After the fall of Gaddafi, Misrata became an important political and military center thanks to its financial influence and the unity of its commercial elite. Politicians from Misrata played a key role in supporting the revolutionary program and were well-represented in the subsequent transitional governments. The leaders of the Misrata brigade pushed for official recognition of their units and for the replacement of the army by ex-revolutionary forces, which was achieved through institutional agreements and budget allocations that secured their power and interests in the security sector (Ben Lamma, 2017, p. 21).

e) Zintan, with the name of a city in western Libya, has a population of about 60,000 people. The Zintani militias control a large territory that links the capital city of Tripoli to the south of the country. It also has control over oil revenues and smuggling profits. Although the Zintani militias fought on opposite sides during Libya's 2019 conflict, they are then united due to a power struggle between the country's two rival prime ministers. Zintan strongly opposes Misrata and the Islamists (Lechner, 2022).

f) Qadhadhfa, an Arab-Berber tribe and one of the Ashraf[6] tribes in the Sirte district of Libya between Tripoli and Benghazi. It is the tribe of the late Libyan president Gaddafi which made it one of the most significant and powerful tribes in the country during the rule of Gaddafi regime. They are now primarily based in the village of Qasr Abu Hadi in Sirte. In 2020, The Qadhadhfa tribe in Libya issued a statement through

---

6　Ashraf are those who are descendants of the family of Prophet Muhammad.

its Social Council, urging all its members to immediately withdraw from the forces led by General Khalifa Haftar. The statement also called on Qadhadhfa members to remove Haftar's mercenaries from the Sirte area (Middle East Monitor, 2020).

g) Tuareg, a nomadic tribe with a significant population of over 500,000 in the Sahara of Libya. They claim several states in the Sahara as their own and have previously attacked other Saharan governments and oil installations in pursuit of independence. However, they did not clash with the Libyan government traditionally, which led to suspicions that Gaddafi had armed them. In 2019, reports have surfaced that the Tuaregs are forming an alliance with the UN-backed Government of National Accord (GNA) to protect southern Libya from the military advances of warlord Khalifa Haftar's militia (TRT World, 2020).

h) Bara'sa, the eastern tribe, which had a majority of high-level administrative positions during the monarchy rule, is the tribe of Gaddafi's second wife, as previously mentioned in this chapter. Thus, many of Gaddafi's children are believed to have supported the tribe, and some members were appointed to mid-level bureaucratic posts. During the uprising, some members of the tribe joined the opposition, while some tribal leaders were hesitant to express their loyalty publicly (CIA, 1987).

i) Si'an, one of the loyal tribes to the Gaddafi regime. Starting in the 1980s, the Gaddafi regime recruited this tribe to serve as border guards, along with other tribes like the Nuwail, to oversee the Libyan-Tunisian border. As a result, the Si'an and Nuwail gained control of smuggling networks for agricultural and construction equipment and materials, using the Nalut route to Tunisia. Amid the 2011 upheaval, local militias accused the Si'an tribe of collaborating with pro-Gaddafi forces. As a consequence, from April to June of 2011, the Si'an were largely displaced. It is noteworthy that on June 24, 2017, the Si'an tribe's spokesman urged Saif al-Islam Gaddafi to take charge of the country following his release earlier that month (European Asylum Support Office, 2018, pp. 3-4).

j) Tebu (Toubou), The Tebu is a non-Arab nomadic tribe that has lived in the Sahara region for a long time across Libya, and other neighboring countries of Chad and Niger. Their numbers are estimated to range from 120,000 to several hundred thousand across these countries. In Libya, their number is about 5.6 million people, representing a small minority group traditionally residing in the southeastern part of the country, specifically in the Tibesti mountains region, near Chad's border. Presently, a relatively large population of Tebu resides in the Al Kufra area of Libya. They have suffered persecution under Gaddafi rule as they faced forced evictions, and displacement from their homes, causing them to scatter across Libya and neighboring countries. Furthermore, there was a decree depriving them of their Libyan nationality (Waas, 2013, p. 5). After the fall of Gaddafi, Tebu's cultural center was established in 2012 to support their rights. (Zurutuza, 2018). The picture in Fig. 3 shows a man of Tebu tripe in his traditional clothes.

Source: (ToubouGa. 2016)

Fig. 3: A man of the Toubou tribe of Libya

k) Zway (or Zuwayya), one of the main Arab Bedouin tribes dominating the Kufra district too. During the initial days of the 2011 revolution, the leader of this tribe played a significant role by expressing support for the protesters as he warned the Gaddafi regime threatening to cut Libyan oil exports to stop oppressing them (Reuters staff, 2011). It's worth mentioning here that the oil production of this district is about 17% of Libya's oil (Grigoriadis & Kassem, 2021, p. 126). The Kufra district dominated by the two tribes of Zway and Tebu has experienced prolonged periods of political, and economic marginalization. Also, this district has suffered many conflicts between the two tribes, resulting in numerous casualties and significant property damage for both groups. Fortunately, in 2018, a Reconciliation Agreement was signed between them ensuring freedom of movement, individual responsibility for offenses, and unbiased access to services in the region (UNSMIL, 2018).

This was a brief introduction to some of those Libyan tribes playing a significant role in the political landscape of Libya throughout history and especially in the civil war and the ongoing situation after the Gaddafi period. Examining the provided brief information for each of those tribes, we can see that they are all involved in the political landscape and in the conflicts to defend their lands and their people's rights.

Tribal influence has its role in every conflict occurring in all regions of Libya. For a simple example, if we look at the Southern region, we can see that it is divided into tribal influential zones, the Tuareg tribe is dominating the western part, and the Tebu is dominating the southern part of Sebha near Kufra. The northern part of the Fezzan region is dominated by Arab tribes. In the district of Sebha, the Arab tribe of Awlad Suleiman is the most influential tribe after the 2011 revolution. The Magarha tribe is mostly dominating the district of Wadi al-Shati. The Zway (or Zuwayya) tribe is dominating most of the Kufra district (Eaton, Alageli, Badi, Eljarh, & Stocker, 2020, p. 35). The location of those districts can be seen in the map of Fig. 4.

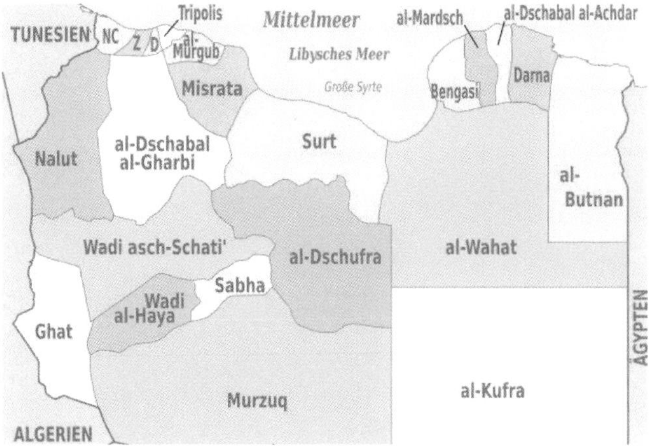

Source: (TUBS, 2012)

Fig. 4: Map of the administrative districts of Libya

Expectedly, due to the absence of strong legal protection for the rights of all citizens, the tribal plurality had led to conflicts that have occasionally developed into civil wars in Libya. This situation has been further complicated by the country's political turmoil, economic instability, and societal divisions, all of which have contributed to the rise of armed groups and the proliferation of weapons. As a result, achieving sustainable peace in Libya has proven to be a formidable challenge, requiring a comprehensive approach that takes into account the country's complex social, political, and economic realities. In light of the challenges described above, the following section of this chapter will examine in more detail those challenges and obstacles facing Libya's tribal plurality while exploring the potential strategies to overcome them and foster a more stable and peaceful future for the country.

IV. Challenges of tribal plurality in the Libyan Society

As previously noted, tribal conflicts can pose significant challenges for societies with a diverse tribal plurality, especially in the absence of a strong, effective government that works to protect the rights of all citizens equally with a fair legal framework. In such cases, including the Libyan case, the lack of legal protections can exacerbate tensions between different tribal groups and undermine social cohesion, potentially leading to further conflict and instability. To address these challenges, it is crucial to promote effective governance, enhance the rule of law, and foster social inclusion, while also addressing the root causes of conflict and ensuring equitable access to economic opportunities.

Examining the situation in Libya throughout history, we can see that Libya had faced a long time of foreign occupation starting with Greeks and Romans in ancient times, followed by Arabs and ottomans in the medieval times, and ended with the Italian colonization in modern era. The tribal plurality can be used in several ways by foreign rulers to enhance their control as usually national unity and coherence threaten the foreign occupiers.

In Libya, efforts to promote national unity and resist foreign rule can be traced back to the Sanusi movement. The movement successfully negotiated with foreign powers and united tribal forces against the Italian occupier. However, this struggle came at a great cost, as the Italian government executed Sanusi military leader Omar al-Mukhtar, who became a national hero for all Libyans (Ryan, 2012, p. 4). Such moments of sacrifice and resistance have strengthened national sentiments and helped to unite the tribes against their enemy represented by the colonizers. In this way, the struggle for independence and national unity remains an enduring part of Libya's history and identity.

The efforts to unify the Libyan tribes and promote national spirit continued after Libya's independence in 1951, with the newly independent state adopting the name "United Kingdom of Libya." Also, Muammar Gadhafi, who belonged to a small tribe, recognized the important role of strengthening national unity against tribalism. However, his regime ultimately failed to achieve this goal. In fact, tribalism increased under his rule, which included persecution of certain tribes, unfair distribution of resources, and inadequate protection of the rights of different tribes that make up Libyan society. These factors contributed to the 2011 revolution and tribalism remains a significant part of Libya's history and identity.

In the aftermath of Gadhafi's fall, Libya faced a chaotic situation as the central government disintegrated. In this power vacuum, one of the major challenges that arose was the need for the diverse tribal groups to maintain peace among themselves. Without a strong central authority to mediate disputes and enforce laws, the potential for conflict and violence among the various tribes increased. This challenge was exacerbated by the fact that some of the tribal groups had taken up arms and were vying for control of territory and resources, leading to further instability and chaos.

In the chaotic and unstable situation that has prevailed in Libya in recent years, issues related to tribal plurality have arisen, particularly those concerning the rights of minorities. One such minority is the Tebu tribe, many members of which were deprived of Libyan citizenship due to historic conflict over the Auzo strip between Chad and Libya in the 1970s. The conflict over the Auzo strip ended in 1994, with Libya ceding the territory to Chad. In 1998, however, the Libyan government issued a decision revoking the Libyan citizenship of all persons born in Aouzo, including many Tebu members. Although this decision was overturned in 2010, its consequences continue to be felt by the Tebu population. As a result of their citizenship status, the Tebu people face difficulties in accessing basic public services such as education and healthcare. In Arab-dominated towns such as Kufra, state institutions like civil registries are often discriminatory towards the Tebu minority. For example, citizenship applications may not be processed, or obstacles may be created due to historic rivalries between the two groups. However, the state has failed to take effective steps to ensure anti-discriminatory measures for minorities, breaching its obligation under Article 8 of the Constitutional Declaration to guarantee the right to education and access to medical care for every Libyan citizen (The Libyan Association for Tebu Culture (LATC), 2014, p. 3).

Furthermore, the Libyan state has neglected the cultural rights of various tribes, including the Tebu, Berbers, and Tuaregh. This includes the preservation of their languages and traditions, which are not specifically protected among the official languages of the state. The neglect of cultural rights represents a further breach of the Constitutional Declaration's obligations to guarantee the preservation of the cultural heritage of every Libyan citizen.

Hopefully, the names of the Libyan governments formed in 2015 and 2021, which are the "Government of National Accord" and the "Government of National Unity," respectively, reflect a growing awareness of the need to address tribalism and promote reconciliation among the conflicting tribes in order to achieve national unity. These names signal a positive step towards stability and peaceful coexistence in Libya. However, the process of achieving lasting peace and unity is ongoing and will require continued effort and commitment from all members of Libyan society.

In a conclusion, we can say that the impact of tribal plurality on Libyan society is significant, creating obstacles to achieving national unity and coherence. The main challenge can be seen in the difficulty in creating a unified national identity which led to continuous tension and competition for resources and power among different tribes. This has been further exacerbated by policies such as favoritism for some tribes and marginalization of others, as well as the neglect of minority rights and cultural heritage. The absence of a central government after the 2011 revolution has only added to the instability and tribal tensions.

Despite the complex challenges posed by tribal plurality, there are still opportunities for Libya to move towards national unity and coherence by implementing more inclusive policies that prioritize the rights of all tribes and their cultural heritage. This requires a fair distribution of resources and power to address past grievances and create a more equitable future for all Libyans.

■ References

Ali, K. H. (2014, Sep.). Maps of tribal, political and jihadist forces in Libya after the revolution (خرائط القوى القبلية والسياسية والجهادية في ليبيا بعد الثورة). *Middle East papers* (مجلة أوراق الشرق الأوسط), 41-55.

Apps, P. (2011, Aug. 25). *Factbox: Libya's tribal, cultural divisions*. Retrieved from Reuters: World News: https://www.reuters.com/article/us-libya-tribes-idUSTRE77O43R20110825

Basu, M. (2011, March 4). *Libya's tribes rise up against Gadhafi*. Retrieved from CNN: http://edition.cnn.com/2011/WORLD/africa/03/03/libya.tribes/index.html

Ben Lamma, M. (2017, Sep. 20). The Tribal Structure in Libya: Factor for fragmentation or cohesion? *Observatoire du Monde Arabo Musulman et du Sahel*, pp. 1-58. Retrieved from https://www.frstrategie.org/en/programs/observatoire-du-monde-arabo-musulman-et-du-sahel/tribal-structure-libya-factor-fragmentation-or-cohesion-2017

Brown, L. C., Buru, M. M., Barbour, N., Cordell, D. D., & Fowler, G. L. (2023, Feb. 9). *Libya*. Retrieved from Encyclopedia Britannica: https://www.britannica.com/place/Libya

CIA. (1987, Nov. 4). *Libya: Tribalism in the Qadhafi Regime*. Retrieved from General CIA Records: https://www.cia.gov/readingroom/docs/CIA-RDP90T001 14R000600580001-9.pdf

Cole, P., & Mangan, F. (2016, Sep. 2). Tribe, Security, Justice and Peace in Libya Today. *Peaceworks*, pp. 1-48.

Cresti, F. (2020). Sulayman al-Baruni in Italy (1919-1920): From the Dream of the Berber Principality to the Italo-Tripolitanian Brotherhood. In A. M. Di Tolla, & V. Schiattarella, *Libya between History and Revolution: Resilience,*

New Opportunities and Challenges for the Berbers (pp. 67-96). Naboli: Unior Press.

Demographics of Libya. (2023, Feb. 4). Retrieved from Wikipedia: https://en.wikipedia.org/wiki/Demographics_of_Libya

Eaton, T., Alageli, A. R., Badi, E., Eljarh, M., & Stocker, V. (2020, March 17). The Development of Libyan Armed Groups Since 2014. *Middle East and North Africa Programme*, pp. 1-66. Retrieved from https://www.chathamhouse.org/2020/03/development-libyan-armed-groups-2014/4-armed-groups-southern-libya

El-Taraboulsi, S. N. (2020). *State Building and State-Society Relations in Libya (1911-1969): An Examination of Associations, Trade Unions and Religious Actors.* Oxford: St. Cross College, University of Oxford.

European Asylum Support Office. (2018, Dec. 14). COI Query Response. Libya: Information on the Si'an tribe. *European Union*, p. https://www.ecoi.net/en/file/local/2003098/LBY_132.pdf.

Fanack Foundation. (2020, Aug. 10). *Population of Libya.* Retrieved from Fanack Chronicle of the Middle East and North Africa: https://fanack.com/libya/population-of-libya/

Grigoriadis, T. N., & Kassem, W. (2021). The Regional Origins of the Libyan Conflict. *Middle East Policy*(28), 119-129.

Harchaoui, J. (2020, July 30). *Tarhuna Mass Graves and Libya's Internationalized civil war/.* Retrieved from Texas National Security Review: https://warontherocks.com/2020/07/tarhuna-mass-graves-and-libyas-internationalized-civil-war/

Hatitah, A. (2011, Feb. 24). *Libyan Tribal Map: Network of Loyalties that will Determine Gaddafi's Fate.* Retrieved from Centre Tricontinental: https://www.cetri.be/Libyan-Tribal-Map-Network-of?lang=fr

Herráez, P. S. (2023). 21st century: the return of tribalism? *IEEE Analysis Paper*, 1-16. Retrieved from https://www.ieee.es/Galerias/fichero/docs_analisis/2023/DIEEEA01_2023_PEDSAN_Tribalismo

IWGIA. (2022, April 1). *The Indigenous World 2022: Libya*. Retrieved from International Work Group for Indigenous Affairs: https://iwgia.org/en/libya/4638-iw-2022-libya.html

Karam, S. (2011, Feb. 22). *Update 1-Factbox-Tribal ties key to Gaddafi rule*. Retrieved from Thomson Reuters: https://web.archive.org/web/20110716000305/http://af.reuters.com/article/idAFLDE71L2K720110222

Kawalya-Tendo, C. (2020, May). *How Dictators Maintain A Stronghold on Power; A focus on Africa's Strongmen*. Claremont: Claremont Lincoln University. doi:10.13140/RG.2.2.35473.79206

Lechner, J. A. (2022, July 16). *Will Zintan Determine Libya's Future?* Retrieved from Foreign Policy: https://foreignpolicy.com/2022/07/16/zintan-libya-militias-tripoli-dbeibah-bashagha-haftar/

Middle East Monitor. (2020, Aug. 28). *Libya: Gaddafi's tribe calls on its members to withdraw from Haftar militia*. Retrieved from The Online Security Sector Observatory: https://www.marsad.ly/en/2020/08/28/libya-gaddafis-tribe-calls-on-its-members-to-withdraw-from-haftar-militia/?doing_wp_cron=1676705230.3069870471954345703125

MRG. (2018, July). *Libya*. Retrieved from Minrority Rights Group International: https://minorityrights.org/country/libya/

Mundy, J. (2021). *Libya: Modern Political History*. Oxford: Oxford University Press. Retrieved from https://doi.org/10.1093/acrefore/9780190277734.013.989

Office of International Religious Freedom. (2022, June 2). *2021 Report on International Religious Freedom: Libya*. Retrieved from United States Department of State: https://www.state.gov/reports/2021-report-on-international-religious-freedom/libya/#:~:text=Sunni%20Muslims%20 represent%20between%2090,of%20whom%20are%20mostly%20foreigners.

PAT Portable Atlas. (n.d.). *Public domain maps of Libya*. Retrieved from PAT maps: https://ian.macky.net/pat/map/ly/ly.html

Raza, S. (2012). Italian Colonisation & Libyan Resistance to the Al-Sanusi of Cyrenaica (1911-1922). *Journal of Middle Eastern and Islamic Studies (in Asia)*, *6*(1), 87-120.

Reuters staff. (2011, Feb. 21). Libyan tribe threatens to cut oil exports soon. *Reuters*, pp. https://www.reuters.com/article/libya-protest-tribes-idAFLDE7 1J0PP20110220.

Ryan, E. (2012). *Italy and the Sanusiyya: Negotiating Authority in Colonial Libya, 1911-1931*. Columbia: Columbia University.

The Libyan Association for Tebu Culture (LATC). (2014, Oct.). *Stakeholder Report to the United Nations Human Rights Council Universal Periodic Review- Libya*. Retrieved from OHCHR: https://uprdoc.ohchr.org/uprweb/downloadfile. aspx?filename=1869&file=EnglishTranslation

ToubouGa. (2016, Sep. 1). *Toubou man traveling*. Retrieved from Wikipedia: https:// eu.wikipedia.org/wiki/Tubu_(etnia)#/media/Fitxategi:Toubou_man_ traveling.jpg

TRT World. (2020, July 21). *Libyan tribes, their loyalties, and Egypt's bait, explained*. Retrieved from TRT World: https://www.trtworld.com/magazine/libyan- tribes-their-loyalties-and-egypt-s-bait-explained-38300#:~:text= Other%20eastern%20tribes%20Sharing%20the%20same%20name%20 as,Italy%20and%20the%20Ottoman%20Empire%20in%20the%20past.

TUBS. (2012, Aug. 9). *Map of administrative divisions of Libya*. Retrieved from Wikimedia: https://commons.wikimedia.org/wiki/File:Libya,_ administrative_divisions_-_de_-_colored.svg

UNSMIL. (2018, Feb. 23). Representatives from the Tebu and Zway tribes reach a Reconciliation Agreement in Kufra. *UNITED NATIONS SUPPORT MISSION IN LIBYA*, pp. https://unsmil.unmissions.org/representatives-tebu-and-zway-tribes-reach-reconciliation-agreement-kufra.

Waas, L. V. (2013, May 24). The Stateless Tebu of Libya. *Tilburg Law School Legal Studies Research Paper Series*, pp. 1-15. Retrieved from http://ssrn.com/abstract=2269569

Worldometers. (2023, Feb. 11). *Libya Population (LIVE)*. Retrieved from Worldometers: https://www.worldometers.info/world-population/libya-population/

Zurutuza, K. (2018, Oct. 13). Tebu cultural awakening: 'We may not be Arabs, but we are Libyan'. *Al-Jazeera*, pp. https://www.aljazeera.com/features/2018/10/13/tebu-cultural-awakening-we-may-not-be-arabs-but-we-are-libyan.

Chapter 5

———

Islamists versus Non-Islamists in Algeria

I. The rise of Islamism in Algeria:

The North African country, Algeria, is the largest in Africa with its area covering 2,381,741 km2 (Saleh, 2022). With this large area, Algeria has a strategic location on the Mediterranean Sea bordering many African countries as seen in the map of Fig. 1. Those countries include the North African countries, Morocco in the west, Tunis and Libya in the east of Algeria. Algeria shares its southern borders with Mauritania, Mali, and Niger.

As we will focus in this chapter on the Islamist and non‑Islamist groups in Algeria, we have to define first the meaning of this concept. "Islamism" or in other word "political Islam" is basically a political ideology striving to derive its legitimacy from the Islamic faith and Islamic law according to their interpretations of Islamic practice and

Source: (CIA, 2021)

Fig. 1: Geographic location of Algeria

tradition. The Islamist movements include Jihadist movements with the extreme form of those groups involved with terror as in the case of Al-Qaeda and the Islamic State in Iraq and Syria (ISIS). Other examples of Islamist movements can be seen in the group conducting the Iran government, and the role of Wahhabism in Saudi Arabia (Zeidan, 2021). Thus, not all Muslims are Islamists while all Islamists are Muslims. Moreover, there are many cases of tension between Islamists and other Muslims opposing them.

Marnia Lazreg, a professor of Sociology, argued in her study on Islamism in Algeria that the roots of those Islamist groups can be traced back to the country's colonial history, which created social and economic inequalities that persisted even after independence. During the colonial period, the French imposed a divide-and-rule strategy, which exacerbated social and economic inequalities between different regions and communities. After independence, the Algerian state attempted to address these inequalities through socialist and nationalist projects, but these efforts were largely unsuccessful. The state's interventionist economic policies, corruption, and lack of democratic participation created a sense of disillusionment among the population, particularly among young people and women. This sense of disillusionment was compounded by the economic crisis of the 1980s, which further eroded the legitimacy of the state. Thus, in this context, Islamism emerged as a political and social movement that offered an alternative vision of society and governance. Accordingly, Islamists criticized the state's policies and called for the establishment of an Islamic state based on sharia law. They also sought to address social and economic inequalities and to provide social services to the population. Briefly, according to this study of Prof. Lazreg, the rise of Islamism in Algeria can be understood as a response to the failures of the post-independence state to address social and economic inequalities, as well as to the country's colonial history and the legacies of that history (Lazreg, 1998, pp. 45-48).

Examining the Islamist groups in Algeria today and tracing their emergence, we can see that the rise of Islamic parties in the early 1990s, such as the popular Islamic Salvation Front (FIS), was fueled by a broad base of support and cohesive hierarchical organization. Though the FIS makeup was diverse, ranging from urban youth to small merchants and civil servants, their vision for governance differed, with the more radical urban youth questioning the role of democracy and leaning towards a minority-led theocracy, while the more moderate merchants and civil servants insisted on an electoral victory for Islamic principles as a culturally authentic way to solve contemporary problems. The subsequent nullification of election results allowed the radical wing of FIS to gain power and dominate its future path, sparking the decade-long civil war that raged from 1991-2002, leaving 150,000 dead. An example of an Islamist group that emerged out of the civil war was the Armed Islamic Group (GIA), which fought in a bloody war against the regime. Even after the end of the civil war in 2002, violent opposition led by Islamist groups persisted in Algeria. The Bouteflika regime was able to negotiate with moderate Islamists and use the security forces to reduce the Islamic resistance to the state. Today, Algerian Islamists can be divided into two camps: regime insiders and terrorists. The regime insiders are Islamists who have been incorporated into the ruling elite while the other camp is defined as terrorists. Despite widespread discontent with the Boutefilka and FLN regime, Algerians have their doubts about political Islam as a solution to their problems (Middle East Policy Council, p. 2015).[1] In

---

1   For more details, see:(Roberts H. , 2003), (Willis, 1996).

the following section of this chapter, we can explore the main groups representing Islamists in Algeria.

II. Current Islamist groups in Algeria:

Algerian law has prohibited political parties based on religion since 1989, but parties with Islamist ideologies still exist in the country. The Movement of Society for Peace (MSP), a moderate Islamist party, was once part of the governing coalition but left in 2012. Despite its subsequent losses in elections, it still operates as an opposition party since 2017. Meanwhile, other Islamist parties are present but face restrictions due to the ban on religion-based parties. The dominance of non-Islamist parties, such as the National Liberation Front (FLN) and the Democratic National Rally (RND) in Algerian politics has limited the influence of Islamist parties on the country's political landscape (Bertelsmann Stiftung , 2022, p. 16). To explore the current Islamist groups in Algeria, we can examine some of the main representative examples, as the following:

II. 1. The Movement of Society for Peace (MSP)

Given that this movement has its roots in the Muslim Brotherhood, we can track its origin by examining the historical context of the Muslim Brotherhood in Algeria. The ideas of the Muslim Brotherhood were introduced to Algeria during the Algerian revolution of the early 1950s against the French colonial forces which had a significant impact on that revolution. The leader of the Algerian branch of the Muslim Brotherhood in 1953-1954, Sheikh Ahmed Sahnoun, emphasized the importance of an Islamic national identity to unite Algerians against the French colonial forces. This concept of national identity played a significant role in the Algerian Revolution enhancing the united front against the Western power. Despite its significant role during the revolution, the Algerian Muslim Brotherhood was marginalized by the National Liberation Front after the conflict. However, the Muslim Brotherhood remains active in religious and educational institutions, where it continues to advocate for a greater political influence of Islam in Algeria. The group gained momentum when it recruited Arabic teachers from Egypt, the birthplace of the Muslim Brotherhood, to reinforce its reformist-Islamist ideologies (Guidère, 2017, p. 320).

In 1990, the Muslim Brotherhood became civically involved in Algeria when the country allowed for a multi-party system. An Algerian cleric named Mahfoud Nahnah, who sympathized with the Brotherhood, converted his religious education and charity organization, called Guidance and Reform, into a political party known as the Movement for an Islamic Society (MSI or Hamas[2]). Nahnah emphasized three principles, including moderation, participation, and gradualism, as he sought to

---

2 "Hamas" is the abbreviation of its Arabic name "حركة مجتمع السلم" pronounced as "Harakat mujtama' as-silm" in English with the same meaning as the movement of Society for Peace (MSP).

establish an Islamic state in Algeria (Boubekeur, 2007, p. 2). But later, religiously oriented political parties were banned, leading to the group's renaming as the Movement for the Society of Peace (MSP). Despite these changes, the group remained a legitimate political organization during the Algerian Civil War and chose not to align itself with the increasingly violent Islamic Salvation Front or the Armed Islamic Group. Today, the Movement for the Society of Peace is considered a moderate Islamist party and has been actively involved in Algerian politics since its inception. The group's leader, Boudjerra Soltani, has been a vocal advocate for democratic reforms and increased political participation, particularly among Algeria's Muslim population (Guidère, 2017, p. 320).

The MSP condemned the use of arms by the Islamic Armed Movement, led by Mustapha Bouyali, considered the founding father of jihadism in Algeria, during the 1980s. In the 1990s, the party attempted to dissociate itself from the Islamic Salvation Front (FIS), which promoted taking control of the government through violent means. Then, the MSP became a member of the Green Algeria Alliance (GAA), which is a coalition of Islamist groups that frequently oppose the Algerian government. They boycotted both the 2014 elections and the 2016 process of constitutional reform. After coming in third in the 2017 parliamentary elections, the MSP accused Bouteflika's ruling coalition of electoral fraud. Abderrazak Makri, the leader of MSP, planned to run for the presidency in 2019 but withdrew after Bouteflika announced he would seek a fifth term which led to protests joined by MSP calling for his resignation and the formation of a caretaker government. Thus, Bouteflika resigned on April 2, 2019, after more than 20 years in power (The Reference, 2020). Briefly, we can say that the MSP has positioned itself as the lead opposition during Algeria's transitional period.

Recently, in January 2023, Makri, the leader of the MSP, met with President Tebboune at the Presidential headquarters and expressed his hope that all parties would work together to preserve the strength of the Algerian State. The MSP's leader welcomed the existence of a relationship between the presidency and the opposition, describing their meeting as civilized and comfortable (APS, 2023). This can be seen as a good sign of convergence between this moderate Islamist group and the government.

II. 2. Islamic Salvation Front (FIS)

This Islamist representative organization is known by its French name, the Front Islamique du Salut (FIS). It is a political and religious organization that originated in Algeria during a period of political liberalization in the late 1980s. The FIS was brutally suppressed by the Algerian army, but it faced an even greater threat from rival Islamist organizations. Despite being an important opposition group in Algeria, ongoing economic concerns and urban uprisings against the ruling class have sidelined the FIS, reducing its influence (Fromherz, 2012).

The FIS was founded by Ali Belhadj and Abbasi al-Madani, known by their Salafi background in 1989. They won the majority of seats in local and national elections in 1990 and 1991, but the government canceled the second round and arrested many FIS members. The FIS then engaged in a long guerrilla war, during which both sides were accused of atrocities. Although the group was accused of assassinating President Mohamed Boudiaf, no conclusive evidence was found. There is some connections between FIS and the Extremist groups of the Armed Islamic Group. Also, Liamine Zeroual, the president of Algeria (1994-1999) attempted to initiate peace talks with the FIS. Despite the unsuccessful outcome of those attempts, Zeroual maintained a willingness to engage in more negotiations conditioned that the FIS renounced the use of violence. (The Editors of Encyclopaedia Britannica, 2020).

According to the program of FIS, it aimed to establish an Islamic state based on Sharia law supported by references from the Quran. The FIS program focused on cultural and religious aspects, which are important for forming an Islamic state, while its economic program favored a market-driven economy that encourages the private sector and global participation in economic activities. The FIS program was subject to criticism for its inadequate commitment to democratic values, as it failed to permit the formation of political parties with differing ideologies, and limited the scope of elections to those conducted solely within an Islamic framework. The idea of democracy led to a split within the FIS because a majority of its members held the belief that Sharia should be the governing law, while others were against the principles of democracy and its associated institutions. However, the military's intervention prevented the democratic option from becoming a reality (Sebastian, 2015, p. 261).

In September 1989, FIS gained legal recognition despite their opposition to a secular state. Thus, their theocratic views clashed with the democratic practices and secular traditions of Algeria led to military intervention in 1992. The FIS received considerable support from the public by adopting a liberator mentality and operating as a quasi-state entity. It positioned itself as a front that aimed to establish justice, create a new state, and take over power. It depicted the government and other political figures as endangering national security and identity. Islamist fervor was widespread in society, but the FIS's transformation during the civil war and its radicalization of social complaints affected its reputation. Although some social groups view the FIS as a victim of a coup, their impact on society is limited today due to the ban on the organization (Zeraoulia, 2020, p. 31).

II. 3. Movement of the Islamic Renaissance (En-Nahda)

Abdallah Djaballah established Jame'iyat En-Nahda (Association of Renaissance) in 1988 in Constantine, an eastern city in Algeria. Two years later, in the autumn of 1990, the association was converted into a political party and was renamed to "the Mouvement de la Renaissance Islamique (MRI)" called shortly "En-Nahda" in Arabic. Djaballah's decision to form En-Nahda was a response to the Islamic Salvation Front's rejection of an Islamic coalition as the FIS's attempt to establish a monopoly on Islamic politics prompted Djaballah to create an alternative party that could challenge their dominance. Thus, the creation of En-Nahda aimed to challenge the FIS's dominance and provide an alternative for Algerians who sought an Islamic political party with a broader base (Tachau, 1994, p. 44).

This movement has faced internal divisions, starting with its founder, Saad Abdellah Djaballah leaving the party in 1999 due to disagreements over collaboration and incorporation into the government. He founded his own party called Harakat el-Islah al-Watani or MRN, and ran for the 1999 presidential elections receiving around 4% of the vote. He also had success in subsequent elections until 2007 when he was ousted from the party's leadership. Djaballah attempted to return to politics by creating a new party, the Front for Justice and Development (FJD), which was later legalized in 2012 as "al-Adala", which means justice in Arabic (Bustos, 2017, p. 208).

En-Nahda and the Movement of Society for Peace (MSP) have always advocated peaceful actions and rejected the radical stance of FIS. En-Nahda has attempted to find a national solution to the illegalization of FIS, and there have been regular contacts and attempts at mediation between the two parties. In this context, we can notice that MSP has maintained cooperative relations with the government, with ministers in every Algerian government since 1997, and is a member of the Presidential Alliance, which supports Abdelaziz Bouteflika's candidacy in presidential elections. In contrast, Djaballah's parties have never held governmental posts or supported Bouteflika, but have held seats in parliament and local/provincial assemblies. En-Nahda participated in the government through the appointment of Abdelwahab Derbal as a minister, and Lahbib Adami as an ambassador for Algeria in Saudi Arabia Adala (Bustos, 2017, p. 215).

II. 4. Armed Islamic Movement (MIA)

The Armed Islamic Movement (MIA) was a reformist group that was considered the first among Algerian Islamists to adopt a military approach as a means to achieve its objectives. Its founder, Mustafa Bouyali was an adherent of Sayyid Qutb, the leading member of the Egyptian. Bouyali had been an outspoken critic of the Algerian government since the mid-1970s before he went into hiding in 1982. He also was influenced by Sheikh Alili, a radical Islamist who left for France in 1986-1987. Bouyali established the MIA as an alliance of small groups. The MIA emerged within the initial violent clash between the government and the Islamists, which took place on November 2, 1982, at the Ben Aknoun university residential complex in Algiers. Following the cancellation of the 1992 Algerian legislative elections, which were poised to result in an Islamist victory, most of the MIA's members, including Ali Belhaj, joined the

Islamic Salvation Front (FIS) and other armed groups (Botha, 2008, p. 29).

In 1992, the Armed Islamic Movement (MIA) was established by two former army officers, Said Mekhloufi and Abdelkader Chebouti who had previously defected to Mustafa Bouyali's armed Islamist group of the same name MIA in the 1980s. The MIA served as the unofficial armed branch of the Islamic Salvation Front (FIS) and was a revival of the previous MIA group. Its creation was believed to be a direct result of the FIS' failure in the political arena. The MIA was reported to have about 1,000 fighters who primarily targeted security forces and low-ranking civil servants. According to Middle East Report, the group's primary objective was to pressure the government to reintroduce radical Islamism into the political process (Roberts H. , July-August 1994, p. 24).

II. 5. Armed Islamic Group (GIA)

The GIA was established in 1989, consisting of several regional groups active in Algiers and the surrounding areas. Initially, the GIA formed a wide-ranging coalition with various armed groups, including Afghan and Algerian veterans, as well as local extremists. However, the death of its leader who brought the groups together led to conflict and violence as the local extremists started to marginalize and even assassinate leaders from other coalition groups. (Thurston, 2020, p. 27).

The group's leader in 1994-1996 was Djamel Zitouni, also known as Abou Abd al-Rahman Amine controlled nine regional leaders or emirs. The GIA began to expand the concept of takfir[3] under Zitouni's predecessors in 1993–1994, punishing civilians who defied its injunctions, including women who refused to wear the hijab, Hairdressers who refused to comply with the order to shut down their businesses, and newsagents who persisted in selling national newspapers. Zitouni went on this further, claiming that the whole of Algerian society had abandoned Islam and should be regarded as apostates. The GIA disintegrated under his leadership as three local emirs refused to recognize his leadership and asserted their independence. Antar Zouabri became the successor to Zitouni after his being assassinated by a faction of the GIA led by Ali Benhadjar. The GIA's extreme conception of takfir was an important element in the much larger massacres of civilians in July–September 1997 and December 1997–January 1998, costing the GIA its ties with the al-Qaeda network (International Crisis Group, 2004, p. 13).

Since its establishment, the GIA claims to be fighting a holy war against government security forces and aims to establish a radical Islamic state in Algeria. It includes former FIS leaders and Algerian guerrilla fighters who fought in the Afghan war. On 26 August 1994, the group announced the establishment of a "caliphate" government in exile in the

---

3 "Takfir" is the Arabic word describing the act of declaring someone an unbeliever, thereby stripping them of their Muslim identity. In contemporary times, this term is also used to justify violent actions against leaders of Islamic nations who are seen as not being devout enough in their religious practices (Takfir, 2023).

United Kingdom. There is limited and contradictory information on the relationship between the GIA and other armed Islamist groups, including the FIS. The GIA claims to be independent of the FIS and has threatened FIS leaders in exile. The FIS denied being involved in the GIA's killing of civilians, but they did not publicly condemn the violence until December 1994. There are conflicting reports on the relationship between the GIA and the MIA. However, The GIA reportedly has good relations with the AIS and frequently cooperates with them. In December 1994, the GIA announced an alliance with the AIS, reportedly approved by the FIS, but some sources claim the document declaring the alliance was false (Immigration and Refugee Board of Canada, 1995). This group declined soon after it was listed as a terrorist organization and a significant number of the GIA's members have either been captured or killed by the Algerian government or have joined other Islamist organizations.

II. 6. Other groups:

The violent confrontation between Algerian Islamists and the Algerian government during the civil war of 1991-2002 involved various armed Islamist militants, some of whom continued to carry out terror attacks after the end of the war, while others disappeared due to the consequences of that long conflict which ultimately ended with a peace accord.

Among those groups dissolved by the end of the civil war, the Islamic

Salvation Army (AIS) was established in the summer of 1994 as the military wing of the Islamic Salvation Front (FIS), with the purported aim of countering and gaining control over the Armed Islamic Group (GIA). Despite being in close contact with FIS leaders, the AIS was operated with a great deal of autonomy and is not necessarily subordinate to civilian leadership. During the 90s civil war, AIS claimed responsibility for various violent acts, including burning schools and killing civilians. Despite this, the AIS has stated its willingness to engage in discussions with the state (Kapil, 1995, p. 5). Eventually, in January 2000, Algerian President Bouteflika issued a general amnesty for all members of the AIS, the military wing of the banned Islamic Salvation Front (FIS), in return for the dissolution of their organization. Also, the AIS had previously committed to returning to the authorities all weapons and other military means and had reached a peace accord with Bouteflika in 1999 (Reuters, 2000). As a result of these measures, the dissolution of AIS can be marked as the beginning of the end of the Algerian civil war that had been ongoing since 1992, bringing a new era of relative stability to the country.

As for other groups, during the Algerian civil war, several Islamist groups defected from the Armed Islamic Group (GIA). This included the Islamic Front for Armed Jihad (FIDA), which split from the GIA in 1993, and the Islamic League for Preaching and Combat founded in 1996, the Houmat al-Da'wa al-Salafyyia, or the Defenders of Salafist

Preaching (HDS), also founded in 1996. Additionally, the Salafi Group for Preaching and Combat (GSPC), founded in 1998 became the most effective among the armed groups in Algeria by 2001 and continued its terror after the end of the civil war, including claiming responsibility for attacks in and outside Algeria (Botha, 2008).

Apart from militant groups, the Sufi brotherhoods in Algeria have gained political significance as the state sees them as a bulwark against extremist ideology and a means to expand its influence. This shift occurred under President Bouteflika, who used Sufi networks to legitimize state policies, mobilize voters, and highlight Algeria's historic religious links to neighboring Sahel countries to expand regional power. As part of this strategy, Bouteflika undertook tours of Sufi lodges (zawiya) across the country, seeking blessings from its leaders, showing reverence at mausoleums, and making financial contributions from state funds in hopes of gaining political backing. Unlike the Salafists, Sufi brotherhoods have become more actively leveraged by the state toward political ends (Sakthivel, 2017).

This observation highlights a common trend across the region, as seen previously in Chapter 3 of this book when discussing Egypt. While Sufi groups have been targeted by extremist Salafis, they have also maintained positive relations with governments. This is particularly evident in the case of Egypt, where Sufis have been able to leverage their influence and historical ties to the state to maintain support and protection.

III. Non-Islamist groups in Algeria

To examine Algerian society, it appears that non-Islamists are the majority. Algeria has a number of political parties that are considered non-Islamist, with a range of ideologies from socialist, liberal, and secular to nationalist. It is worth noting that religiously oriented political parties are prohibited in Algeria. Furthermore, the Algerian government has had a lengthy conflict with Islamists, which has affected society. In addition to political parties, labor unions also play a significant role in Algerian politics. The General Union of Algerian Workers (UGTA), the largest and oldest trade union in Algeria, represents workers in various sectors. Since the UGTA has been linked with the ruling National Liberation Front (FLN) party, it can be considered non-Islamist.

In this context, it should be mentioned that UGTA leader Abdelhak Benhamouda played a role in preventing the rise of Islamism by establishing the National Committee to Safeguard Algeria (CNSA). The committee aimed to combat religious extremism and uphold the values of the Republic. It demanded that the electoral process be halted, leading to the resignation of the President, the discontinuation of the electoral process, and the dissolution of the Islamic Salvation Front. The UGTA supported Liamine Zéroual in the first pluralist presidential elections of independent Algeria in 1995 and continued its political commitment after his victory. Abdelhak Benhamouda contributed to launching a mass political party to support the President's program and actions but was assassinated by a terrorist group in 1997 (Djabi, 2020, p. 10).

Algeria's civil society organizations also constitute an essential element of the non-Islamist group. These organizations, which include human rights groups, environmental groups, women's groups, and youth groups, usually advocate for human rights, democracy, and social justice. They play a crucial role in holding the government accountable, and their principles often differ from those of Islamists who usually criticize them.

Furthermore, during the Algerian civil war, there were reports that stated the Algerian government's security forces supported armed groups that were against Islamists and were responsible for issuing numerous death threats against suspected Islamists. Among those groups was the Organization of Young Free Algerians (OJAL), which began its operations in 1993 and claimed to aim at eliminating terrorism. Those operations of OJAL included kidnapping and killing supporters of FIS. In response to an incident in which an Islamist killed a young girl who was not wearing the Islamic veil (hijab) in February 1994, OJAL announced that it would kill 20 veiled women and 20 bearded Islamists for each woman killed for not wearing the hijab. Accordingly, within a month of this announcement, OJAL carried out this threat by killing two high school students who were wearing the veil near Algiers. Despite the many death threats and violent actions carried out by OJAL against Islamists and their supporters, the Algerian government did not condemn OJAL's actions (Amnesty International (AI), 1994, p. 19).

Other anti-Islamist groups would include also Berbers (Amazigh). Around 17 to 25 percent of Algeria's population are Berbers, with the Kabyles being the main group. They reside in Kabylia in the northern part of the country and have been less impacted by the conflict than other regions. Despite being Arabized, Berbers have maintained their distinct culture, and the Berber Cultural Movement (MCB) was created to preserve it. The MCB is actively struggling for Tamazight, the Berber language, to be recognized as an official language and introduced in schools. The Kabylia region has experienced sporadic armed Islamist incursions, and Berber political leader Said Saadi has organized local self-defense groups in response. The two primary Berber political parties, the RCD and FFS, both oppose establishing an Islamic republic in Algeria (Immigration and Refugee Board of Canada, 1995). The following picture of Fig. 2 shows protestors raising the Amazigh flag during the anti-government protests in 2019.

Another part of the non-Islamist sector is Algerian intellectuals and artists who have contributed to the country's cultural and political landscape. Some of these intellectuals and artists have been criticized and threatened by Islamists for their attitudes, which violate Islamic principles.[4] Also, the Algerian business community, which includes local

---

4 This can be seen clearly during the Algerian civil war as the targeted individuals were often prominent members of society, including intellectuals, journalists, civil servants, and other professionals. These individuals were singled out for their perceived opposition to the armed

Source: (Al-Jazeera, 2019).

Fig. 2: Algerian Berbers participating in protests of 2019

entrepreneurs and foreign investors in various sectors, such as oil and gas, agriculture, and manufacturing, is another part of the non-Islamist sector. They often advocate for economic liberalization and profit-making, without concerning themselves with religious issues.

Briefly, the majority of Algerian society is comprised of non-Islamist groups, including political parties, labor unions, civil society organizations, Berbers, intellectuals, artists, and the business community. This would be due to the traumatic experiences endured by the Algerian

Islamist groups or for their perceived support of the government. Many writers and political activists who called for the cancellation of the 1992 elections or wrote against the political agenda of the FIS and the armed Islamist groups were also targeted. This systematic targeting of intellectuals and professionals had a devastating impact on Algerian society and contributed to a culture of fear and intimidation (Amnesty International (AI), 1994, p. 19).

people during the period when Islamists held political power. This resulted in a protracted civil war characterized by numerous terror attacks and an ongoing conflict between the government and the Islamists. Consequently, the Islamists lost popular support and garnered a negative reputation among the Algerian population.

IV. An overview of the Islamist and non—Islamist Rift in Algeria

Upon examining Algeria's political landscape since gaining independence, it becomes apparent that after a prolonged fight against foreign colonization, Algerian society desired to establish a new era that honors their culture with its strong Islamic roots. As a result, Islamism emerged as a powerful movement in Algeria, with a persistent focus on implementing Islamic principles in all aspects of life, including political practice. Other segments of Algerian society, particularly those in political power, did not welcome the emergence of Islamism. This resulted in a political power struggle between Islamist and secularist groups, leading to a prolonged civil war that lasted over a decade and further widened the divide between Islamists and non-Islamists in Algeria.

The political practice showed that both the Islamist and secularist groups often refer to the FLN's declaration on November 1, 1954, which aims to establish an Algerian state based on Islamic principles while being democratic and socially responsible as there is a lack of recognition that the original statement was vague and open-ended. This recognition is necessary for a truly democratic debate on the role of Islam as the official religion and how Algeria can establish a state based on the rule of law. The conflict between Islamism and secularism, as well as between the Islamist movement and the state, has polarized and hindered the political process. The army's decisions in 1992 confirmed and deepened this blockage, resulting in the neglect of substantial issues concerning the construction of a state governed by law, the establishment of representative government, and the promotion of private enterprise in non-oil manufacturing sectors, which were not adequately tackled by Algerian politicians for more than ten years after the collapse of the one-party system (International Crisis Group, 2004, p. 22).

Following a long conflict between Islamist groups and the Algerian state, the army agreed in 2003 to stop interfering in politics, and in 2008, the limit on presidential terms was lifted. However, the 2016 constitution reversed this by reinstating term limits and strengthening the legislature. In 2019, millions of Algerians supported the Hirak, a pro-democracy movement, due to high levels of corruption and deteriorating living conditions (see the picture of Fig. 3). This movement showed a decrease in societal divisions as evidenced by the unity of the population during the Hirak marches and inter-regional networks supporting political detainees. Throughout the 54 weeks of protests, the

Source: (Mezahi, 2021).

Fig. 3: Mass Algerian Protestors in Hirak demonstrations

army remained peaceful, and the influence of small numbers of Islamist guerrillas declined, with few attacks reported. The Algerian army also reported a decrease in the number of armed fighters eliminated in 2020 compared to 2018 (Bertelsmann Stiftung , 2022).

This decline in the Islamist role during the Hirak movement demonstrated that these groups have lost support from the local population. As for the Islamist political parties, they showed low electoral support, and although they publicly claim to support democratic goals and market liberalization, their role was weak during the Hirak movement. Yet, some online activists with substantial followings support these parties. On the other hand, there are a few anti-democratic radical Islamist groups that operate in the Sahara and eastern regions, and external interference from IS actors has increased the potential threat of these groups (Bertelsmann Stiftung , 2022).

In conclusion, considering the traumatic period of the 1990s civil war, we can observe that the Islamist movement in Algeria has lost much of its support. As a result, their influence has declined both politically and socially. On the other hand, the majority of Algerian society, composed of non-Islamists, has shown greater solidarity and efforts to build trust among themselves, as evidenced by the various initiatives during the Hirak movement, such as public clean-ups campaigns, voluntary medical aid responders, and sharing Ramadan meals. These efforts have continued during the Covid-19 pandemic, further strengthening the unity and convergence of Algerian society.

◼ References

Al-Jazeera. (2019, July 29). *Algeria. the release of the Amazigh flag-raisers* (الأمازيغ الجزائر.. الإفراج عن رافعيْ راية). Retrieved from Aljazeera Center for Public Liberties & Human Rights: https://liberties.aljazeera.com//الأماز-رابة-الجزائر-الإفراج-عن-رافعيْ/

Amnesty International (AI). (1994). *Algeria: Repression and Violence Must End.* London: Amnesty International.

APS. (2023, Jan. 4). *President Tebboune receives leader of Movement of Society for Peace.* Retrieved from Algeria Press Service: https://www.aps.dz/en/algeria/46307-president-tebboune-receives-leader-of-movement-of-society-for-peace

Bertelsmann Stiftung. (2022). *BTI 2022 Country Report — Algeria.* Gütersloh: Bertelsmann Stiftung .

Botha, A. (2008). Terrorism in Algeria. In *Terrorism in the Maghreb: The transnationalisation of domestic terrorism* (pp. 23-83). Institute for Security Studies.

Boubekeur, A. (2007, May). *Political Islam in Algeria.* Brussels: Centre for European Policy Studies.

Bustos, R. (2017). Algerian Islamism: Analysis of Elites and Resources in Major Political Parties and Social Movements (1990-2016). In F. I. Brichs, J. Etherington, & L. Feliu, *Political Islam in a Time of Revolt* (pp. 203-226). Palgrave Macmillan Cham.

CIA. (2021). *Algeria.* Retrieved from The World Factbook 2021, Central Intelligence Agency: https://www.cia.gov/the-world-factbook/countries/algeria/map

Djabi, N. (2020). *Trade unions in Algeria: History, Survey and Options.* Fredrich Ebert Satiftung.

Fromherz, A. (2012, July 24). *Islamic Salvation Front (FIS).* Retrieved from Oxford

Bibliographies: https://www.oxfordbibliographies.com/display/document/ obo-9780195390155/obo-9780195390155-0215.xml

Ghanem, D. (2015, April 14). *The Future of Algeria's Main Islamist Party*. Retrieved from Malcolm H. Kerr Carnegie Middle East Center: https://carnegie-mec. org/publications/?fa=59769

Guidère, M. (2017). *Historical Dictionary of Islamic Fundamentalism*. Lanham: Rowman & Littlefield.

Immigration and Refugee Board of Canada. (1995, June 1). *Islamism, the State and Armed Conflict*. Retrieved from Refworld: https://www.refworld.org/ docid/3ae6a8228.html

International Crisis Group. (2004, July 30). Islamism, Violence and Reform in Algeria: Turning the Page. *ICG Middle East Report*(29).

Kapil, A. (1995, January/February). Algeria's Crisis Intensifies: The Search for a 'Civic Pact'. *Middle East Report, 25*(1), pp. 2-7.

Lazreg, M. (1998). Islamism and the Recolonization of Algeria. *Arab Studies Quarterly, 20*(2), 43-58. Retrieved from http://www.jstor.org/ stable/41858247

Mezahi, M. (2021, Feb. 20). *Algeria's protests are back and the president is worried*. Retrieved from BBC: https://www.bbc.com/news/world-africa-56128140

Middle East Policy Council. (n.d.). *A History of Islamist Movements in Algeria*. Retrieved from Teachmideast: https://teachmideast.org/articles/a-history- of-islamist-movements-in-algeria/

Reuters. (2000, Jan. 11). *Algeria grants full amnesty to Islamic rebels*. Retrieved from CNN: http://edition.cnn.com/2000/WORLD/africa/01/11/algeria. amnesty/index.html

Roberts, H. (2003). *The battle for Algeria: Sovereignty, health care, and humanitarianism*. Pennsylvania : University of Pennsylvania Press.

Roberts, H. (July–August 1994). Algeria Between Eradicators and Conciliators. In *Middle East Report* (pp. 24–27). Washington D.C.: Middle East Research & Information Project.

Sakthivel, V. (2017, Nov. 2). *Political Islam in Post-Conflict Algeria.* Retrieved from Hudson Institute: https://www.hudson.org/national-security-defense/political-islam-in-post-conflict-algeria

Saleh, M. (2022, Aug. 17). *Largest countries in Africa 2020, by area.* Retrieved from statista: https://www.statista.com/statistics/1207844/largest-countries-in-africa-by-area/

Sebastian, N. (2015, Sep.). Islamic Movements Engaging with Democracy: Front Islamique Du Salut (FIS) and the Democratic Experiment in Algeria. *India Quarterly, 71*(3), 255–271. Retrieved from http://www.jstor.org/stable/45072757

Tachau, F. (1994). *Political parties of the Middle East and North Africa.* Westport: Greenwood Press.

Takfir. (2023, March 24). Retrieved from Oxford Reference: https://www.oxfordreference.com/view/10.1093/oi/authority.20110803101936564

The Editors of Encyclopaedia Britannica. (2020, August 4). *Islamic Salvation Front.* Retrieved from Encyclopedia Britannica: https://www.britannica.com/topic/Islamic-Salvation-Front

The Reference. (2020, March 20). *Muslim Brotherhood in Algeria.* Retrieved from The Reference: https://thereference-paris.com/10653

Thurston, A. (2020). Algeria: The GIA from Incorporation to Tyranny. In *Jihadists of North Africa and the Sahel: Local Politics and Rebel Groups* (pp. 27–62). Cambridge: Cambridge University Press.

Willis, M. (1996). *Politics and power in the Maghreb: Algeria, Tunisia and Morocco from independence to the Arab Spring.* Oxford: Oxford University Press.

Zeidan, A. (2021, Aug. 26). *Islamism*. Retrieved from Encyclopedia Britannica: https://www.britannica.com/topic/Islamism

Zeraoulia, F. (2020). The Memory of the Civil War in Algeria: Lessons from the Past with Reference to the Algerian Hirak. *Contemporary Review of the Middle East, 7*(1), 25–53.

Chapter 6

Evolving Islamic Concepts in Tunisia: Navigating Tradition and Modernity

I. A Historical Overview of Tunisia's Religious Landscape

Tunisia is located in North Africa between Algeria and Libya, as seen in the following map of Fig. 1. Throughout history, Tunisia's proximity to Italy across the Mediterranean made it an attractive target for European invaders throughout history including the Romans who ruled the region from 146 BCE until the Arab Muslim conquest in the 7th century. The most recent European occupation of Tunisia was by the French, who occupied the country from 1881 until Tunisia gained its independence in 1956 (The Editors of Encyclopaedia Britannica, 2020).

During the early Islamic period, Tunisia was known as Ifrīqiyyah, which is derived from the Roman word for Africa. The region was shortly ruled by the Vandals and then the Byzantine Empire before it was conquered by the Arab Muslims in the year 647 CE. After the

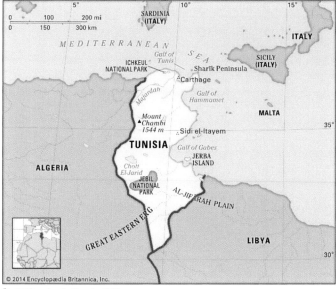

Source: (Encyclopædia Britannica, 2014).

Fig. 1: Geographical Location of Tunisia

Arabs initially unified North Africa, a separate Tunisian dynasty was established by Andalusian Muslim Amazigh called "Ḥafṣids" in the thirteenth century. Later in 1574, Tunisia became a part of the Ottoman Empire till the 19th century. By that time, the vast majority of Tunisia's inhabitants spoke Arabic, with Berber surviving in only a few pockets. The population was predominantly Muslim with a small Jewish minority. Tunisia was the smallest of the Maghreb states, making it more easily controlled from within, and more open to outside influences. Thus, it was intensively Christianized under Roman rule and then Islamized during the long Islamic rule (Barbour, Brown, Clarke, Murphy, & Talbi, 2023).

Thus, throughout history, Tunisia has experienced significant shifts in its religious and cultural landscape. Similarly to other North African countries, the religious status of the Tunisian people changed from a majority of Christianity which was the dominant religion under Roman rule, but with the arrival of Muslims in the 7th century, Islam became the majority religion. Then, in modern times, during the French occupation (1881-1956), the Tunisian people experienced another significant cultural shift as the French culture was imposed on them. This was particularly evident in the French colonial policy of Education, which aimed to assimilate Tunisians into French culture and values.

Education played an important role during those cultural shifts throughout the history of Tunisia. Religious education dominated Tunisia for centuries, with the Medersa of the Al Zaytouna Mosque serving as the primary source of education since its creation in 737, until the establishment of the first non-religious, military school in 1838, and subsequently the first modern, non-religious, and non-military educational institution, the Sadiki College, in 1875. Despite the emergence of modern educational institutions, the traditional elementary education offered in the traditional Quranic schools called Kottabs remained prevalent in 1893 with a total of 961 Kottabs (Ben Salah, Chambru, & Fourati, 2022, p. 3).

As for European education in Tunisia, it began in the early 19th century with the arrival of European migrants. We can see that it also started with religious institutions seeing the establishment of the first Protestant school for the Maltese population and the first Israeli school by the London Jews Society in 1830. The first French school was established in 1840 earlier before the French occupation, followed by a dozen more French and other European private schools in Tunisia's main cities until 1883. However, it was only after France enacted Jules Ferry's laws in 1881, that French public schools became free, compulsory, and secular (Ben Salah, Chambru, & Fourati, 2022, p. 4).

As a result, French education had an impact on the religious and cultural landscape in Tunis by forming a new French-educated elite influenced by Western secular education more than Islam. This impact can be seen in the attitude of the Tunisian ruling elite after independence, which adopted secular policies and banned some Islamic features. These policies will be discussed in more detail in the following sections of this chapter.

II. Tunisia's Changing Islamic Landscape

Tunisia is well known for its rich Islamic history, but it is also known for its strong secular traditions. The country's religious landscape has been shaped by various political changes, which at times have supported the separation of religion and state, while at other times have emphasized an Islamic identity. In the wake of the 2011 Arab Spring uprisings, which began in Tunisia, the country's political landscape has undergone significant changes, with corresponding effects on its Islamic landscape.

The evolution of Islamic concepts in Tunisia can be attributed to the influence of secular governments, which have been in power since the country's independence and until the 2011 revolution. Thus, the Tunisian governments tended to restrict religious fundamentalism through many measures. This can be seen in the secular policies taken under the rule of the first Tunisian president after the independence, Habib Bourguiba, who was known as one of the most strongly secular political leaders in the Arab world. He made significant changes to the laws governing religious endowments, education, and the legal system in Tunisia. He worked towards unifying the legal system so that all Tunisians, regardless of their religious beliefs, were subject to the state courts.

Also, Bourguiba sought to diminish the impact of the religious University of Ez-Zitouna by incorporating a theology faculty into the University of Tunis as a replacement. Additionally, he made members of the religious hierarchy into state employees and implemented regulations for the expenses associated with maintaining mosques and paying preachers (Ayubi, 1991, p. 113). The policy implemented by the Tunisian government affected several Islamic concepts, including polygamy, which was prohibited under the 1956 Code of Personal Status, despite being permitted in Islamic law (Murphy, 2023). It's worth mentioning that only Tunisia and Turkey are banning polygamy among Muslim countries.

Moreover, among the Islamic countries, or countries with an Islamic majority of the population, Tunis was the only Arab country that banned the Islamic head cover (hijab) for a long period of its history which ended recently after the 2011 revolution. In the following image of Fig. 2, Tunisian President Habib Bourguiba can be seen during a public gathering in the streets of Tunisia in 1957, removing the traditional hijab worn by Tunisian women in attendance. This event illustrates the initial efforts to challenge the Islamic concept of the hijab in Tunisia, which began soon after the country's independence.

Source: (Lindsey, 2017)

Fig. 2: President Bourguiba removing the hijab of a Tunisian woman

Banning hijab was legally applied despite the fact that the vast majority of 98% of the Tunisian population is Sunni Muslim. In 1981, a law was enacted prohibiting women from wearing the Islamic head cover (hijab) in public offices, while Decree 108 of 1985 forbids hijabs in educational institutions. Enforcement of these regulations was renewed in the early 1990s and once again in 2006. Despite these measures, the wearing of hijabs has become more prevalent, particularly among young working women and students, who regard it as a symbol of freedom. In 2008, a lawsuit was won by lawyer Saida Akremi on behalf of a schoolteacher who contested the prohibition of wearing a hijab at work. Nevertheless, the effects of the decision have been minimal due to the country's unwillingness to implement it uniformly because of its polarizing nature (Freedom House, 2010).

Banning the hijab lasted since 1981 and continued during the long-time rule of the Tunisian President Zine al-Abidine Ben Ali. Thus, with the fall of his rule by the 2011 revolution, the Islamic hijab and even the more extreme version (niqab) covering the face was re-allowed (Abdelhadi, 2006). Then, in 2019, the niqab was banned in government offices by the Tunisian Prime Minister Youssef Chahed due to security reasons relative to the terror suicide bombings repeatedly occurred three times in the Tunisian capital in that week (BBC News, 2019). The changing policies in Tunisia reflect the evolution of the country's Islamic landscape, which has been influenced by shifting political dynamics over the past decade. This includes the period during which an Islamic party was in power.

That Islamic party is Ennahda Party, known in English as the

Renaissance Movement Party, which was illegal during Ben Ali's rule and emerged as the most organized rival of the old regime after the 2011 revolution. Thus, this Islamic party won the election 90 seats of the total 217-member Constituent Assembly with nearly 70 % of the voters. In 2013, following the assassination of two secularist politicians that caused division and instability in Tunisia, the Ennahda party relinquished power to a caretaker government. They collaborated with the secularist Nida Tounes party to draft a new constitution that accommodated both Islamist and secularist interests, which took effect in 2014. Ennahda supported a unity government led by Nida Tounes after the ensuing parliamentary election. However, in the 2019 parliamentary election, Ennahda lost 17 seats but won the most seats, while Tunisia faced economic and corruption-related issues. Ennahda initially supported President Kais Saied but a constitutional crisis erupted in January 2021, leading to protests in July and the suspension of parliament by Saied. Ennahda opposed Saied's actions strongly. Ennahda, along with other significant political players in Tunisia, was not part of the constitutional reform talks during Saied's administration. As a result, the party refused to participate in the referendum on the proposed changes in July 2022, which was successfully passed without any hindrance. Furthermore, Ennahda opted not to nominate any candidates for the parliamentary election held in December 2022. (The Editors of Encyclopaedia, 2023).

This change in political power had an impact on the modification of the Tunisian laws concerning Islamic concepts. In this context, in 2018, the Tunisian cabinet approved a bill requiring the equality of inheritance shares for males and females. This would made Tunisia the first again among Arab countries to violate Islamic rule in this regard (Sadek, 2018). The issue of gender equality in Tunisia has been a contentious topic since 2018 when the late President Caid Essebsi supported the recommendations for gender equality in inheritance proposed by the Commission for Individual Freedoms and Equality. Although women's rights activists praised this move, it caused a rift within the centrist camp and drew condemnation from conservatives and Islamists, leading to Caid Essebsi's political isolation. The debate resurfaced in 2020 when President Kais Saied expressed his opposition to gender equality in inheritance. During a National Women's Day event, he criticized discussions around gender equality in inheritance, calling them a "false debate" and suggesting they were not innocent. He claimed that the Quranic text does not allow for any interpretation in this matter and that the principle of inheritance in Islam is based on justice and equity, rather than formal equality (Zayat, 2020). The following image of Fig. 3 shows The Tunisian President in that speech on the National Women's Day in Carthage palace in 13 August 2020.

Fig. 3: President Kais Saied's speech on National Women's Day

Another debate about the change of the Islamic concepts in Tunisia rose concerning the Islamic identity of the country. This can be seen in the modification of the constitution. In 2014, the Tunisian constitution was adopted, demonstrating the success of the Tunisian case in achieving a civilian democratic transition after the 2011 revolutions and confirming that Islam is its religion clearly. However, Tunisia has experienced many crises with the rise of radical Islamic currents to Parliament in 2019. Later on, the 2022 Tunisian constitution has been a subject of controversy since its release. Critics have raised objections to its provisions relating to identity and religion, particularly the change from Islam being the religion of the state in former constitutions of Tunisia to the state being a part of the Islamic nation and obligated to work towards achieving the purposes of Islam in the new constitution of 2022. This has raised doubts that the constitution's provisions may be used to limit religious freedom, especially the right of minorities to practice their religion freely. This could lead to restrictions on freedom of belief. Additionally, civil society groups have criticized the new constitution for undermining the principle of a balance of powers and limiting the prerogatives of the legislative and judicial branches (Hafnaoui, 2022). On the other hand, this modification raised fears about the impacts of removing Islam as the religion of Tunisia and the intention to remove all references to Islam in Tunisian laws as clearly declared by the Tunisian Presidents who adopts secular policies.

Briefly, we can say that the shifting political power between secularist and Islamist groups has impacted Tunisian society, raising concerns about the implementation of political ideologies in policies that either align with Islamic or non-Islamic trends. This can summarize the analysis of the changing Islamic landscape in Tunisia seen in the last decades. Another factor behind the evolution of Islamic concept within the Tunisian society can be seen in the Westernization which will be the focus of the following section.

III. The Influence of Westernization on Islam in Tunisia

During the 75-year-long French occupation, Western thought seeped into Tunisian society. The French culture permeated the education system, prioritizing the French curriculum and encouraging Tunisian elites to study in France. This is evident in the education background of the first Tunisian president, Habib Bourguiba, who graduated from the law faculty in Paris, and the second Tunisian president, Bin Ali, who received military training in France and studied Engineering in the United States.

The long period of Western occupation has left Tunisian society divided into two main groups. One group, consisting of the urban high and middle classes who had access to Western education, became modernized and was well represented in the post-independence government due to their education. The other group, which comprised the lower classes of Tunisian society, living mainly in rural areas and villages, were not able to access modern Western education due to their low social status and difficult economic conditions. Consequently, they preserved their traditional Arabic and Islamic beliefs. As a result, it was not surprising that the educated upper classes who were Westernized led the political control after independence, and thus spread their Westernized values and practices over traditional ones.

Since independence, emigration has played a significant role in shaping Tunisia's population. The majority of the first wave of emigrants were Europeans, with the vast majority departing during the 1950s and 1960s. According to census data, the number of foreign residents decreased from over 341,000 in 1956 to less than 67,000 in 1966 and under 38,000 in 1975. Furthermore, the Jewish community in Tunisia has significantly declined and almost disappeared (Berry & Rinehart, 1986, p. 80).

On the other hand, a considerable number of Muslims have migrated, mostly for temporary employment overseas. Between 1966 and 1975, about 19,000 Tunisians emigrated annually. However, this trend decreased in the mid-1970s due to changes in the economy which resulted in decreased demand for foreign labor. In 1983, an estimated 300,000 Tunisians were residing in foreign countries, which was a decrease from 350,000 in 1979. Western Europe was the preferred destination, where approximately 180,000 Tunisians lived in France exclusively in 1981. Additionally, many Tunisians migrated to Libya to seek employment, given the economic benefits from the oil price increases in the 1970s (Berry & Rinehart, 1986, p. 81). The persistent migration of Tunisians to Europe, particularly France, has enhanced the relationships between Tunisia and the West, and likely contributed to the ongoing Westernization of Tunisian society as migrants impact their families and friends in Tunisia.

The 1984 census revealed that nearly half of the national population (47%) were urban residents. This proportion had remained stable since 1975, but had increased significantly since 1966 (40%) and 1956 (30%). Urban localities were defined as administrative communes with populations of 2,000 or more inhabitants. The growth of cities and towns accelerated in the post-independence years due to the increasing migration of rural people. Between 1966 and 1975, the urban population grew at an average annual rate of 4.2%, compared to only 0.5% in rural areas. However, this gap narrowed in the following nine years to 3.0%

and 2.0%, respectively (Berry & Rinehart, 1986, p. 82). These facts are important to be mentioned seeing that Urbanization and Westernization can be closely linked, as the growth of urban centers often leads to adopting Western cultural values and practices by those who move to the city seeking economic opportunities and a modern way of life.

Another impact of the Westernization with the penetration of French culture through education can be seen in the language spoken by Tunisians. Besides the official Arabic language, French is commonly used and continues to play an important role in Tunisia after its independence, particularly in the Tunisian press, education, and government. Many Tunisian academic scholars even prefer to use French than Arabic in their research writings or lectures. In many academic events, I met Tunisian Professors adopting this trend. Moreover, the French language has even influenced Arabic, resulting in a unique Tunisian dialect that blends many French words into the language.

The debate over the role of the French language in Tunisian society continues to be a complex and contested issue. Some argue that the continued use of French in education and the media perpetuates a form of cultural colonization and hinders the development of a strong national identity rooted in Arabic and Tunisian culture. However, others see the ability to speak French as a valuable skill in the globalized world and recognize the importance of maintaining ties with France and the wider French-speaking world for economic and cultural reasons.

This strong French influence and the deep relations with France since independence can explain the incident of the Tunisian parliament's rejection of demanding a French apology for the crimes of the French occupation in Tunis. In 2020, Tunisia's parliament rejected a motion presented by the opposition Al-Karama party which demanded an apology from France for the crimes committed against the Tunisian people during and after French colonial rule while requesting fair compensation for the victims of French actions. The motion also accused France of supporting tyranny and dictatorship in Tunisia. However, only 77 votes were cast in favor of the motion, falling short of the required 109 votes of the total 217 members needed for it to pass (Salmi, 2020).

Generally observing Tunisian society, we can note that the impact of Westernization on Tunisian society is evident in the adoption of Western-style clothing and social behaviors that run counter to Islamic teachings. One notable example is the legal consumption of alcohol in Tunisia, which is prohibited by Islam. In comparison to other Muslim countries, Tunisians are among the highest consumers of alcohol. According to the World Health Organization (WHO), Tunisia has the highest rate of alcohol consumption in the Maghreb region (MWN, 2014). The Westernized lifestyle observed in Tunisian society is comparable to that of other North African countries, such as Egypt, which were also influenced by long periods of European occupation, as discussed in detail previously in this book.

Old documentaries and films of Tunisian society demonstrate this Westernized lifestyle, which emerged since the rise of the Tunisian republic in the mid-20th century. The following pictures of Fig. 4 can summarize the Westernized lifestyle seen in the contrast between the Westernized dining scene of an upper-class family and a lower-class family preserving old traditions as illustrated in the first Tunisian Movie after the independence.

Source: A Screenshot of the Tunisian movie "Al-Fajr" (Khlifi, 1966).

Fig. 4: The Contrast of the lifestyle of Westernized upper class and lower class in Tunisia as documented by the Tunisian cinema

The first image in Fig. 4 shows a wealthy family dressed in European-style clothing reflecting the woman more liberated, gathered around a dining table with chairs that are also in a Western style. In contrast, the second image depicts a Tunisian family eating in a modest rural house, following the traditional custom of gathering around a knee-high round table. The clothing worn by this rural family is more traditional, with one of the men wearing a traditional outfit and both women more modestly dressed, with their heads covered.

Talking about Tunisian movies, it is noteworthy to mention that the introduction of cinema and filmmaking in Tunis was brought about by France as the French Lumière brothers shot a series of documentary films in Tunis during 1896 and 1897 which was the first filming experience in Tunis (Sunya, 2021). This highlights another way in which Westernization impacted Tunisian society through the introduction of Western-made mass media similarly to other countries influenced by the Western media especially among young generations.

IV. Islamic and Traditional Practices in Modern Tunisian Society

The Tunisian society has undergone a long process of Westernization, as previously discussed in this chapter. Despite the development of many modern aspects in Tunisian society, especially among the upper classes and urban areas, many traditional practices still persist, notably in rural areas and among Islamists and conservatives. When we say here "traditional," it does not necessarily refer to Islamic practices, as some traditional practices violate Islamic norms. For example, in rural areas, the traditional view of land possession as a family honor has an impact on the implementation of inheritance laws, resulting in the deprivation of women's legitimate rights to inherit lands provided by Islamic law.

As despite the ongoing debate over gender equality in inheritance and attempts at legal reforms previously mentioned in this chapter, inheritance is still determined in Tunisia by Islamic Shari'a law, which grants a son double the share of a daughter and a husband double the share of a wife. However, in the real application in Tunisia and similarly, in other Arab countries as well, the unequal treatment of women with respect to inheritance especially in rural regions even extends beyond what is mandated by the Islamic law. In some cases, women do not receive their allotted share of inherited land or real estate. In other cases, even when women receive their share, men still control the land or other properties.

This issue is rooted in Tunisian and similar Arab societies regardless the religion. It is further compounded by social norms that attach a sense of honor to familial ownership of land, which is traditionally held as collective property to avoid dividing it by inheritance. Also, due to the traditional view of women as being controlled by their husbands, there is a fear of losing land to other families if women receive their inherited shares. Thus, in rural Tunisia, women often work on the land but have little control over it. Moreover, the lack of transparency in the inheritance process further exacerbates the problem.

Sometimes, efforts to take away the land that women inherited can have unintended consequences, as seen in the central coastal Sahel region of Tunisia. In the past and until the 1960s, female relatives were given land there that was of saline with poor quality, but now that area is in high demand for tourism development and thus has become the subject of many legal disputes as male heirs claim the right of those lands after decades of giving them to female heirs (Tanner, 2020). All these incidents are based on social traditions violating Islamic law that gives women the right of receiving their inheritance and have full control of their properties.

Another tradition practiced in Tunisian society is monogamy, which was legally established through the 1956 Code of Personal Status, banning polygamy in Tunisia. This tradition of monogamy is not common in the Muslim world, especially in early times, as Islam allows polygamy which was prevalent before Islam. Tunisians have been practicing monogamy since the early centuries of Islamic history. The tradition is based on the 'Kairouan dowry', a form of marital contract that strongly confirms women's rights. The story of the 'Kairouan dowry' dates back to the eighth century when the future Abbasid caliph, Abu Jaafar Al-Mansour, sought asylum in Kairouan and then married a Tunisian lady named Arwa, who then became the mother of his son Al-Mahdi, the third Abbasid caliph. Arwa who was the first wife of caliph Al-Mansour insisted that he would not marry another woman while she was his wife. This was recorded in a pre-nuptial agreement known as the 'Kairouan dowry'. Even after becoming the Abbasid Caliph, Abu Jaafar al-Mansour remained committed to this agreement until Arwa's death. The Kairouan dowry also included provisions for inheritance and endowments as Arwa established the first female Wakf (endowment) and passed down her farm called 'Al-Rahba' only to her female descendants (Al-Arabiya English, 2017).

In fact, this tradition of monogamy does not contradict Islam, as the Prophet Muhammad himself did not allow his nephew Ali bin Abi Taleb to marry a second wife while he was married to the Prophet's daughter Fatima.[1] Islam permits polygamy to regulate a pre-existing practice that was widespread before Islam, but it also imposes conditions on it, such as the requirement of justice between wives and the limitation of the number of wives. However, this does not mean that Muslim women are prohibited from requiring monogamy from their husbands, and if such an agreement is made, husbands are obliged to fulfill it in accordance with the Islamic principles of upholding commitments and promises.

The issue of Muslim women marrying non-Muslims is another distinctive aspect of Tunisian Islamic concepts that sets it apart from mainstream interpretations of Islam. In 2017, President Beji Caid Essebsi of Tunisia made a call for the government to abolish the prohibition on marriages between Muslim women and non-Muslim men, which

---

1 Among the hadiths of Prophet Mohammad reporting this is the following hadith narrated by Al-Miswar bin Makhrama: "I heard Allah's Messenger (ﷺ) who was on the pulpit, saying, "Banu Hisham bin Al-Mughira have requested me to allow them to marry their daughter to `Ali bin Abu Talib, but I don't give permission, and will not give permission unless `Ali bin Abi Talib divorces my daughter in order to marry their daughter, because Fatima is a part of my body, and I hate what she hates to see, and what hurts her, hurts me" (Hadith No. 5230 of Sahih al-Bukhari).

had been enforced since 1973 arguing for its being against Tunisia's constitution adopted in 2014 after the revolution. As a result of his initiative, the ban was lifted, and Tunisian Muslim women were granted the right to choose their spouses, even though it faced opposition from mainstream Muslim clerics. Previously, Muslim women in Tunisia were not permitted to marry non-Muslim men, whereas Muslim men were allowed to marry non-Muslim women according to Islamic law (Al-Jazeera, 2017). Expectedly, the decision has been hailed as a victory for women's rights by secular and liberal groups in Tunisia, but it has been condemned by Tunisian Islamists and conservatives. Tunisia's decision to lift the ban on Muslim women marrying non-Muslims makes it a unique case among Muslim countries, as such marriages are commonly prohibited in other Muslim countries.

Away from those debatable cases, Islamic practices are evident in the Tunisian society despite its western and modernized appearance. This can be seen in the religious activities of the mosques and other Islamic institutions spreading over the Tunisian lands, and the struggle of many women to keep their Islamic custom of hijab or even niqab which is subjected to legal restrictions as previously mentioned in this chapter.

There are concerns about the potential spread of extremist ideology through the Islamic education provided by various Islamic associations and unofficial Quranic schools that lack government oversight on the curriculum. It is important to note that in the Tunisian capital, there are approximately 1,800 Quranic schools affiliated with the Ministry of Religious Affairs, as well as around 600 Quranic schools affiliated with the Tunisian League for the Defense of the Holy Qur'an, 300 Islamic Quranic associations, and 600 Quranic schools associated with charitable organizations, in addition to other independent Quranic schools. Following the 2011 revolution, Quranic education in Tunisia has been divided into three categories: formal education through traditional Kottabs, semi-formal education through the Tunisian Association for the Preservation of the Noble Qur'an, which operates under state control, and non-official education through numerous associations that focus on Quranic studies and memorization, which are spread throughout Tunisia. In 2022, some reports stated the approximate number of students enrolled in these Quranic schools, institutes, and associations in Tunis alone is around 55,000 (Hadwi, 2022). The increase of Islamic education has raised concerns among secular Tunisians, particularly regarding the potential spread of extremist ideology and its possible effects on terrorism.

The 2021 Country Reports on Terrorism in Tunisia, released by the US Department of State, show a decrease in the frequency and scale of terrorist attacks carried out in the country. This positive development is attributed to educational programs implemented by Tunisian ministries and civil society organizations, which aim to prevent the radicalization of Tunisian society. The efforts also involve cooperation with the US on counterterrorism measures. In October 2021, the U.S. Agency for International Development initiated the MA3AN program, a 5-year, $48 million program focused on enhancing community resilience and preventing violent extremism at both community and national levels (Bureau of Counterterrorism, 2021).

A general observation of Tunisian society reveals that Islamic practices in Tunisia vary depending on the Islamic thought embraced by different Muslim groups, such as liberal Muslims, Sufis, Salafis, and extremists. This highlights the diversity present among Muslims in this North African country, which is the central focus of this book.

V. Impact of Tunisia's Muslim Diversity on Islamic Concepts

In light of the information discussed in this chapter, it can be concluded that Tunisian society, like many other North African countries, has been shaped by a long history of exposure to foreign cultures. This has resulted in a unique combination of modern and traditional aspects that are present throughout Tunisian society. The most recent foreign occupation, in particular, has had a significant impact on the country, as it brought with it a strong influence of French culture that deeply impacted a society that had been Arabized and Islamized for centuries prior. As a result, there is a unique blend of various groups with diverse thoughts that have been influenced by both Islamic and Western cultures.

In a manner similar to the variation of Muslims in Egypt previously introduced in the third chapter of this book, Tunisia also presents various Islamic groups, which can be observed through women's clothing indicating their stance as liberal Muslims, conservatives, or extremists. Moreover, there is a significant presence of Sufis in Tunisian society, seen in their Sufi lodges and activities, which are supported by the state due to their representing the peaceful model of Islam in addition to their connection with traditional folklore and thus their impact on tourism.

In contrast with Sufis who tend to avoid politics, another prominent Muslim group in Tunisia is the Islamists who actively engage in the political sphere. Among them, the Ennahda movement stands out as the most notable, having played a crucial role in all government coalitions in the decade following the Tunisian revolution. However, their influence has waned in recent years due to the emergence of more secular forces in positions of power.

These diversities among Tunisian Muslims are influenced by various factors, such as their level of education, their degree of acceptance of Westernization, and their different interpretations of Islamic teachings and practices. Therefore, we can distinguish between liberal Muslims who tend to follow a more flexible approach towards Islam, and Sufis following a more spiritual and mystical interpretation of Islam.

On the other hand, Salafis are known for their strict adherence to the literal interpretation of the Quran and Hadith, which can lead to conservative and often extremist views. Extremist groups, such as the Islamic State and Al-Qaeda, have also gained some traction in Tunisia, especially after the Arab Spring in 2011, which resulted in a power vacuum and political instability in the country.

Despite the differences in Islamic practices, Tunisian society has generally been known for its moderate interpretation of Islam, which has contributed to the country's relatively stable and peaceful social and political environment. However, the rise of extremist groups and the spread of extremist ideologies have become a concern for the Tunisian government and civil society organizations, who have been working to combat radicalization and promote a moderate interpretation of Islam.

Efforts have been made to promote educational programs and initiatives that foster critical thinking, dialogue, and tolerance toward different beliefs and opinions. These programs aim to prevent the spread of extremist ideologies and promote social cohesion and integration, which are crucial in maintaining Tunisia's stability and security.

In conclusion, it can be inferred from this chapter that the development of Islamic concepts in Tunisian society was primarily shaped by the Westernization and modernization policies implemented by the government during and after the colonial period. Tunisia's efforts towards modernization were reflected in the country's approach to Islamic concepts such as polygamy, religious education, and the status of women.

The first president of independent Tunisia introduced reforms to limit the influence of religious authorities and promote modernization, including the secularization of education, modernization of the legal system, and promotion of women's rights. Subsequent governments implemented additional reforms, such as the prohibition of the niqab in public institutions. The Tunisian approach towards Islamic concepts is unique in the Arab world and is regarded as a model for other countries that aspire to balance modernity and tradition in a democratic and human rights-centered context.

The unique model presented by Tunisia regarding the evolution of Islamic concepts in Tunisian society highlights the country's commitment to modernity, democracy, and human rights. Tunisia's progressive approach towards religion, particularly the role of Islam in society, is a result of a series of historical, social, and political factors. The country's modernization project, which started with independence from France in 1956, aimed to transform Tunisia into a modern, secular, and democratic nation-state. This project included significant reforms in education, law, and politics, which affected various aspects of Tunisian society, including religion.

■ References

Abdelhadi, M. (2006, Sep. 26). *Tunisia attacked over headscarves.* Retrieved from BBC News: http://news.bbc.co.uk/2/hi/africa/5382946.stm

Al-Arabiya English. (2017, Sep. 10). *How Tunisian women inspired monogamy in Islam centuries ago.* Retrieved from Al-Arabiya News: https://english.alarabiya. net/perspective/features/2017/09/10/How-Tunisian-women-inspired-monogamy-in-Islam-centuries-ago

Al-Jazeera. (2017, Sep 14). *Tunisia lifts ban on Muslim women marrying non-Muslims.* Retrieved from Al-Jazeera: https://www.aljazeera.com/news/2017/9/14/ tunisia-lifts-ban-on-muslim-women-marrying-non-muslims

Barbour, N., Brown, L. C., Clarke, J. I., M. E., & Talbi, M. (2023, Apr. 29). *History of Tunisia.* Retrieved from Encyclopedia Britannica: https://www.britannica. com/place/Tunisia/History

BBC News. (2019, July 5). *Tunisia bans niqab in government buildings.* Retrieved from BBC News: https://www.bbc.com/news/world-africa-48888144

Ben Salah, M., Chambru, C., & Fourati, M. (2022, May). The Colonial Legacy of Education: Evidence from Tunisia. *Working Paper Series.*

Berry, L., & Rinehart, R. (1986). The Society and Its Environment. In H. D. Nelson, *Tunisia: A Country Study* (pp. 71-144). Washington D.C.: Foreign Area Study series, The American University.

Bourguiba and the Pioneering of Women's Rights بورقيبة وريادة حقوق المرأة (2020). *Pavement ink* حبر ع الرصيف. Alghad TV. Retrieved from https://www. youtube.com/watch?v=YUEVcKgBWWc

Bureau of Counterterrorism. (2021). *Country Reports on Terrorism 2021: Tunisia.* Retrieved from US. Department of State: https://www.state.gov/reports/ country-reports-on-terrorism-2021/tunisia

CIA. (2021). *Algeria.* Retrieved from The World Factbook 2021, Central Intelligence Agency: https://www.cia.gov/the-world-factbook/countries/algeria/map

Encyclopædia Britannica. (2014). *Physical features of Tunisia.* Retrieved from Encyclopædia Britannica: https://www.britannica.com/place/Tunisia

Freedom House. (2010, March 3). *Women's Rights in the Middle East and North Africa 2010 - Tunisia, .* Retrieved from UNHCR-Refworld: https://www.refworld.org/docid/4b99011cc.html

Hadwi, K. (2022, June 19). *Parallel religious education raises an ongoing debate in Tunisia* (التعليم الديني الموازي يثير جدلا متواصلا في تونس). Retrieved from Al-Arab: https://alarab.co.uk/التعليم-الديني-الموازي-في-تونس-يثير-جدلا-متواصلا

Hafnaoui, R. M. (2022). *Implications of the Role of Religion in Tunisia's New Constitution for Non-Muslims Movement in Tunisia.* Retrieved from Religious Freedom Institute: https://religiousfreedominstitute.org/implications-of-the-role-of-religion-in-tunisias-new-constitution-for-non-muslims-movement-in-tunisia/

Khlifi, O. (Director). (1966). *The Dawn (Al-Fajr)* [Motion Picture].

Lindsey, U. (2017, July 10). *Some Gains, Many Sacrifices: Women's Rights in Tunisia.* Retrieved from Al-Fanar Media: https://www.al-fanarmedia.org/2017/07/scholars-debate-legacy-state-feminism-chances-overcoming-islamist-secularist-divide/#google_vignette

Murphy, E. (2023, Apr. 2). *Habib Bourguiba.* Retrieved from Encyclopedia Britannica: https://www.britannica.com/biography/Habib-Bourguiba/Presidency

MWN. (2014, Dec. 25). *WHO: Tunisians, Heaviest Alcohol Drinkers in the Region.* Retrieved from Morocco World News (MWN): https://www.moroccoworldnews.com/2014/12/148071/who-tunisians-heaviest-alcohol-drinkers-in-the-region

Sadek, G. (2018, Dec. 4). *Tunisia: Cabinet Approves Bill Requiring Equal Inheritance Shares for Men and Women.* Retrieved from Library of Congress : https://www.loc.gov/item/global-legal-monitor/2018-12-04/tunisia-cabinet-approves-bill-requiring-equal-inheritance-shares-for-men-and-women/

Saleh, M. (2022, Aug. 17). *Largest countries in Africa 2020, by area.* Retrieved from statista: https://www.statista.com/statistics/1207844/largest-countries-in-africa-by-area/

Salmi, Y. (2020, June 10). *Tunisia lawmakers reject motion on French colonial rule.* Retrieved from Anadolu Ajansu: https://www.aa.com.tr/en/africa/tunisia-lawmakers-reject-motion-on-french-colonial-rule/1871602

Selim, K. (Director). (1939). *Al-Azeema (The Will)* [Motion Picture]. Retrieved from https://www.dailymotion.com/video/x8ew3by

Sunya, S. (2021). Worldly Matters: Distributed HIstories of Tunisian Amateur Cinema and the Screening of Nontheatrical Film. In M. Salazkina, & E. Fibla-Gutiérrez, *Global Perspectives on Amateur Film Histories and Cultures.* Bloomington: Indiana University Press.

Tanner, V. (2020). *Strengthening Women's Control Over Land: Inheritance Reform in Tunisia.* Retrieved from DAI: https://dai-global-developments.com/articles/strengthening-womens-control-over-land-inheritance-reform-in-tunisia/

The Editors of Encyclopaedia. (2023, April 20). *Ennahda Party.* Retrieved from Encyclopedia Britannica: https://www.britannica.com/topic/Ennahda-Party

The Editors of Encyclopaedia Britannica. (2020, May 2). *Tunisia summary.* Retrieved from Encyclopedia Britannica: https://www.britannica.com/summary/Tunisia

Zayat, E. (2020, Aug. 14). *Tunisian president rejects gender equality in inheritance.* Retrieved from The Arab Weekly: https://thearabweekly.com/tunisian-president-rejects-gender-equality-inheritance

Chapter 7

Diversity of Sufi Muslims in Morocco

I. Features of the Moroccan Muslim Society

Located in the furthest northwestern corner of Africa, Morocco was the last North African country to be conquered by Muslim Arabs during the eighth century, specifically in the year 709, under the authority of the Umayyad Caliphate. Being a part of North Africa, the indigenous people of Morocco were the Amazighs (Berbers). While they showed resistance to the Arab Muslim conquest, they predominantly adopted Islam. However, they persisted in rebelling against Arab rule, which is evident in their uprisings during the 740s, and later achieved success in establishing small independent states within Moroccan territories. Subsequently, Islam spread throughout Morocco under the governance of various dynasties, including Arabs like Edrisids, as well as Berbers like the Almoravids, Almohads, and Marinids, persisting as a Muslim kingdom up to the present day. Unlike other North African nations that fell under the dominion of Arab Muslims, Morocco did not come under Ottoman rule, in spite of the Ottoman Empire's efforts in the 16th century to annex Morocco into its realm. Since the 17th century, the Alawite dynasty of sharifs has stood as the final ruling dynasty in Morocco, maintaining its position up to the present day. In the 20th century, Morocco witnessed phases of European occupation by both France and Spain before gaining independence in 1956. It is noteworthy that Spain continues to control the enclaves of Ceuta and Melilla within Moroccan territories, so these coastal areas remain under Spanish rule till today.[1] The map in Figure 1 shows Morocco's location close to Spain, with the Spanish ruled cities of

Source: (Encyclopædia Britannica).

Fig. 1: Geographic Location of Morocco

---

1   For more details on Morocco's history and the Arab conquest of Morocco, see: (Hitti, 1996), (Swearingen, Miller, & Laroui, 2023).

Ceuta and Melilla situated on Morocco's northern coast.

According to the statistical data of 2022, the Moroccan population is about 36.7 million. Islam is the religion of the Moroccan state with more than 99% of the Moroccan population being Muslim Sunni, while less than 0.1% are Muslim Shi'a, and the rest of population include small minorities of Christians, Baha'is and Jews. Muslims in Morocco predominantly adhere to the Maliki School of jurisprudence, which is formally recognized and adopted within the country. Moroccan law stipulates that publicly funded educational institutions are required to provide instruction on Sunni Islam in accordance with the teachings and traditions of the Maliki School.[2] The Moroccan constitution designates Islam as the state religion and guarantees freedom of religious practice. Religious institutions, led by the Ministry of Islamic Affairs, oversee religious affairs and education (Office of International Religious Freedom, 2022, pp. 2-4). The vibrant call to prayer echoing from countless minarets and the bustling activity during religious festivals like Ramadan reflect the deep-seated Islamic culture in Morocco similar to other Islamic countries of the North African region. Moreover, Morocco's geopolitical location at the crossroads of Africa and Europe has imbued its Islam with cultural influences from both regions, contributing to a distinctive Moroccan

---

2 Maliki School is one of the main four Sunni Schools of Islamic jurisprudence. It was founded in the 8th century following the teachings of the Muslim legist of Medina, Imam Malik Ibn Anas (Britannica, The Editors of Encyclopaedia. 2018).

Muslim identity that is characterized by tolerance, pluralism, and an embrace of religious diversity.

II. The emergence of Sufism in Morocco

Sufism, the mystical dimension of Islam, is practiced by various Muslim groups through different approaches known as "Tariqa" or "order". The term "Sufism" has several possible origins. It could come from the Arabic word 'suf صُوف,' referring to the woolen clothing worn by Sufis as a symbol of their ascetic lifestyle. "Sufism" is also linked to 'Safaa صَفاء ,' meaning purity in Arabic, or 'Suff صَفّ,' which means bench or line, referencing the early Sufis who used to sit on a bench within Prophet Muhammad's mosque during the early years of Islamic history. Another potential root is the Greek word 'Sofia' meaning 'wisdom' (Mubarak, 2012, p. 53). These various roots contribute to the rich meaning "Sufism", which is embraced by numerous groups within the Muslim world as a means of self-purification aimed at attaining divine closeness. Nevertheless, Sufi ideology doesn't find universal acceptance among Muslims, as a significant number view these beliefs as heretical groups or deviations from the true path of Islam.

As for the situation in Morocco, Sufism has experienced a profound rise, weaving its spiritual tapestry into the cultural fabric of the nation. Rooted in the early Islamic period, Sufism's growth in Morocco gained momentum with the establishment of numerous Sufi brotherhoods and Sufi lodges like "zawayas" and "ribats", which flourished during the medieval era. Over time, Sufism's influence expanded across Moroccan society, fostering a unique blend of religious devotion and communal solidarity.

Sufism was introduced to Morocco later than other parts of the Muslim world taking shape in the country roughly a century following its emergence in other places like Muslim Spain. Notably, during the 12th century, the Almoravid movement, followed by the Almohads, played a key role in spreading Sufi ideals in the region.[3] Morocco witnessed the emergence of numerous charismatic Sufi saints who not only impacted the Sufi scene within the country but also left their influence on other parts of the Muslim world. One notable figure is Abu Madyan Al-Ghawth, who moved from Al-Andalus to live Morocco in the 12th century. Also, among the Moroccan Sufi saints, there's Sidi Abu l-Hasan Al-Shadhili, along with other prominent Sufis, who attracted many devoted followers, making Sufism more significant in the region. After the Almohads, the Marinids, another Berber dynasty that ruled Morocco until the fifteenth century, played a significant role in fostering the growth of Sufism within the country. They provided substantial support to Sufi leaders and their zawiyas, contributing to the flourishing of

---

3   For more details, see: (Cornell, 2010).

Sufism in Morocco (Trimingham, 1988, pp. 46-50).

Similar to various regions in the Muslim world, Sufism's beginnings in Morocco can be traced back to the individual endeavors of some devout individuals aiming to reach a deeper connection with the divine. Subsequently, some people chose to follow this path, dedicating themselves to the same spiritual journey of those initial Sufi pioneers in order to achieve a heightened closeness with God. Thus, what starts as individual practices within Sufism eventually evolves into collective practices, resulting in the formation of groups that honor these paths. These groups are influenced by individuals regarded as Sufi saints and ultimately give rise to a variety of distinct Sufi orders.

One of Morocco's Sufi pioneers was Abd al-Salam Ibn Mashish, a figure from the 13th century known as the "pole of the west". This title refers to his role in initiating a distinct form of Moroccan Sufism in the western Islamic world, characterized by unique characteristics that set it apart from the Sufism that emerged in the east. He was the Sheikh 'mentor' of Abul-Hasan Al-Shadhili, the founder of the widely practiced Shadhili Sufi order in Morocco (Rodríguez Mediano, 2016).

Sufi orders have often played crucial roles in Morocco's social and political landscape. The spiritual aspects of Sufism have strongly resonated with Moroccans, somehow fostering spiritual strength and social unity. Despite contemporary challenges, Sufism maintains enduring influence, adapting to new contexts while preserving its essence in Morocco.

Various Sufi institutions provide diverse activities for their followers. The upcoming section of this chapter will explore these aspects in more detail shedding the light on the diversity of the Sufi orders in Morocco.

III. The diversity of Moroccan Sufi orders

In this part, we will delve into the diverse Sufi orders present in Morocco, providing an introduction to some of the key ones. Mostly, influenced by the early Sufi leader Abu Madyan Al-Ghawth who is recognized as the master of the 12th century Sufis not only Morocco but also within the entire western Sufism of the Maghreb region. Based on Abu Madyan teachings, many various Sufi orders were established by his disciples including Abd al-Salam Ibn Mashish, who wielded considerable influence within the landscape of Sufi orders in Morocco. Notably, among Mashish's disciples was the founder of the renowned Shadhili order, which holds a preeminent position as the most significant Sufi order throughout the North African region. Thus, we will introduce three of the main Sufi orders in Morocco starting with this Sufi order of Shadhiliya. Furthermore, we'll take a brief glance at other Sufi orders that contribute to the rich tapestry of Sufism in Morocco. By examining these Sufi orders, we can observe the deep connections among different Sufi orders in Morocco, revealing their interdependence and the emergence of numerous sub-orders stemming from them.

1. Shadhili Order:

Named after its founder, Sheikh Abul-Hassan Al-Shadhili from the 13th century, the Shadhili Sufi order originated. He was born in Ghumara, located near Cueta in northern Morocco. He pursued studies in the foundations of Islamic Law (fiqh) at the Qarawiyyin University in Fez and and later passed away in Egypt. His life was marked by journeys to various countries, one of which was Iraq, where he encountered Sufi Shaykh Wasiti and was deeply influenced by their meeting. Afterward, he returned to Morocco to seek guidance from Sheikh Abd al-Salam Ibn Mashish, who became his spiritual mentor, and he embraced his teachings. Later on, Shaikh Al-Shadhili ventured from Morocco to Spain and eventually found his settled abode in Alexandria of Egypt.[4]

The name "Al-Shadhily" became associated with him due to his extended stay in Shadhla, a small town on the outskirts of Tunis, during his pilgrimage journey. The legitimacy of the Shadhili Order stems from its foundation on adhering to the teachings of the Quran and Sunnah while seeking a reconciling between Sharia and spiritual truth. The founder of this path made it clear that its commitment doesn't entail a monastic lifestyle or detachment from worldly needs. Instead, it represents a middle path, advocating moderation in all aspects of life, whether material or spiritual, and rejecting misguided

---

4　For more details, see: (Al-Mālikī. 2023).

Sufi deviations. The Shadhili practices is deeply rooted in remembrance of God (dhikr), particularly through affirming "There is no god but Allah" and sending blessings to Prophet Muhammad. Importantly, the founder didn't mandate having a spiritual guide, enabling seekers to progress independently. He also didn't require involvement in specific religious settings. This Sufi order expanded widely across the Islamic world and served as the cornerstone for various Sufi Sufi branches, with some evolving into as many as nineteen distinct sub-orders. Among these, the Jazuliyya and Zarqawiyya orders hold notable prominence (Mohammed VI Foundation of African Oulema, 2019).

Established in 2010, a union of the Mashishi Shadhili zawayas was formed to unify not only the various Shadhili orders within Morocco but also worldwide. This union is based on their essential connections, stemming from the influential teachings of Sheikh Abd al-Salam Ibn Mashish, who mentored Sheikh Al-Shadhili. It is noteworthy that the Shadhili order in Egypt asserts itself as the original, citing the location of the founder's mausoleum in Egypt, while Moroccan Shadhilis refer to it as Mashish Shadhili, reaffirming its connection to Ibn Mashish, whose mausoleum is situated in Morocco (Badreldin, 2014).

Related to this context regarding the main Shadhili lodges in Morocco, although the founder of this order's mausoleum is located in Egypt, the primary mausoleum and zawiya of the order are associated with Sheikh Abu Mohammad Salih al-Majiri. He was among the closest disciples

Fig. 2: Mausoleum of Sidi Abu Mohammad Salih al-Majiri

of Al-Shadhili during his presence in Morocco. This zawiya, known as Al-Majiriya, is located in the port city of Safi along Morocco's Atlantic coastline (El-Resala, 2020). The Majiriyyun Sufi order derived from his teachings which was based on the Abu Madyan Al-Ghawth's traditions as he himself was also one of the disciples of Abu Madyan (Trimingham, 1988, p. 51). The image in Fig. 2 shows the Mausoleum of Sidi Abu Mohammad Salih al-Majiri inside this zawiya.

2. Qadiri Boutchichi order

The Qadiriya order, believed to be the oldest Sufi order, traces its origins to the Ḥanbali theologian, Sheikh Abdel Qadir Al-Jilani (1078-1166 A.D.), who was born in Iran and passed away in Iraq. His interpretation of Sufism revolved around a spiritual struggle or 'jihad' against one's personal desires, aiming to conquer egoism and worldly attachments and to surrender to the divine will. The Quadiriyya order was further propagated by his son to expand across North Africa, Central Asia, and India. This order, emphasizing qualities such as philanthropy, modesty, devotion, and temperance, maintains a loose structure, allowing each local community to develop its unique ritual prayers (dhikrs) (The Editors of Encyclopaedia, 2023).

The Qadiriyya order was introduced to Western Africa during the 15th century by immigrants coming from the Toat region in the southwestern Algerian desert or Al-Andalus who established their first center in Fez, Morocco, and from there, their influence spread to different regions, leading to the emergence of many sub-orders as well (Al-Qaderi, 1979, p. 48). The name of this order developed by the 19th century adding "Boudchichiyya" naming after one of its sheikhs, Sheikh Sidi Ali bin Mohammed, who was known as "Sidi Ali Boudchich" due to his practice of providing people with a simple dish called "Ad-Dashisha" during times of famine at his zawiya . This dish, made from ground barley, is a well-known basic food in Morocco and other North African countries (Hammad, 2016).

Today, this Sufi order is based in the village of Madagh, located in eastern Morocco near the Moroccan-Algerian border. The Image in Fig. 3 shows the main Boudchichi zawiya in Madagh. It's well-known for organizing two annual gatherings that attract over 250,000 attendees.

Fig. 3: The Boudchichiyya Qadiriyya Zawiya in Madagh, Morocco

The first event is held on the 27th night of Ramadan, which many Muslims believe to be a significant night, while the second occurs on the Prophet Muhammad's birthday. The teachings of this Sufi order indicate deep respect for the spiritual leader "the sheikh" considering the relation between him and his fellows like the relation between the doctor and the patient who should follow the doctors' instruction well. Thus, the follower is also required to have complete faith in the sheikh's ability to provide guidance and direction. Moreover, they must regularly engage in reciting the unique supplications of this Sufi order (Al-jazeera, 2017). In this aspect, we can note that this order differs from the Shadhili order, which allows for more flexibility in these practices.

Starting from the 1970s, the Boutchichi Sufi order has spread widely within Morocco's educated middle class thanks to the initiatives of Sheikh Sidi Hamza, its then leader. With the support of the Moroccan authorities, established a meaningful presence in both diplomatic and political spheres. Its expansion has been notable in recent decades, with its followers numbering around 100,000 by 2009. The backing of the Moroccan Monarch has notably influenced this order, showcasing its activities through state media channels. Setting itself apart from conventional Sufi orders, the Boutchichi order has effectively embraced contemporary tools like magazines, websites, and dedicated spokespersons to update its approach for today's world. Also, it downplays certain Sufi practices considered outdated, such as visiting saints' graves for blessings. Sheikh Sidi Hamza has limited many religious obligations, making adherence more accessible and flexible for modern and professional supporters. He emphasizes enjoying life as one sees fit and visiting the zawiya when desired, as proximity eliminates impurity (Fakir, 2021, pp. 129-130).

The Boutchichi order also organizes an annual international forum for Sufism under the sponsorship of the Moroccan king.[5] This highlights the significant role that this Sufi order is attempting to fulfill, establishing

---

5 The 17th session of that forum was held on 5-10 October 2022, in partnership with the Euro-Mediterranean Center for the Study of Islam "CEMEIA" under the slogan "Sufism and the question of action: of reform from the individual to the construction of society" (Euromagreb, 2022).

connections with Sufis not only inside Morocco but also worldwide.

3. The Tijani order

Originating in Fez, Morocco, in 1781, the Tijaniyya Sufi order, established by Aḥmad al-Tijani, who followed another Sufi order of Khalwatiyah before, has gained a significant presence across northern and western Africa as well as the Sudan (The Editors of Encyclopaedia, 2021). The name of this Sufi order originates from the Berber tribe 'Tijania,' to which the founder of the order belongs through his maternal lineage. Tijani was an Algerian with Moroccan ancestry, born in Ain Madhi, a town in the Algerian province of Alaghouat. His Moroccan great-great-grandfather, originally from the town of Safi in Morocco, immigrated and settled in Ain Madhi, where he married a woman from the Tijania tribe. His first visit to Fez was in 1758, during which he met with Sufis belonging to various other orders. This experience had a significant impact on him, leading him to follow some of those Sufi orders such as the Nassiriyah, Seddiqiyah, and Qadiriyah. In 1772, he started his pilgrimage journey to Mecca. In his way, he met the Sheikh of the Khalwatiyah order, which prompted him to emprace this Sufi path. During his pilgrimage route through Tunis and Egypt, he met with several Sheikhs of the Khalwatiyah order before finally reaching Mecca in 1773 (Tidjania Order, 2020).

In the town of Boussemghoun, situated in Algeria's El Bayadh Province,

Tijani experienced a vision where he saw the prophet Muhammad. In this vision, he was instructed to initiate a new Sufi order. This marked the turning point for him, leading him to break away from his previous affiliations with other Sufi orders. In 1781, he established the Tijaniyya order, which gained prominence in the Boussemghoun region, where he resided for approximately fifteen years. Later, in 1796, he moved to Fez, Morocco, from where he further spread his Sufi order (Abun-Nasr, 1965, p. 37).

In Fez, Tijani was welcomed by Mawlay Sulayman, the Sultan of Morocco by then, who favored him as a Sufi leader compared to other Sufi groups. The Moroccan Sultan provided him with a residence and designated him as a member of his council of scholars. Tijani selected the Mawlay Idris Mosque for his regular prayers, while conducting the rituals of the Tijani order in his home. Eventually, Tijani established his own zawiya to be the center of spreading the teachings of his order which expanded rapidly to become the largest in West Africa (Abun-Nasr, 1965, p. 17). The image in Fig. 4 shows this zawiya where his mausoleum also exists.

Unlike other Sufi traditions, Al-Tijani claimed a direct connection to Prophet Muhammad, without a traditional lineage. His claimed link with the Prophet involved direct instructions in the form of 'dhikr' for divine remembrance. In contrast to other Sufi circles, visiting shrines or tombs of saints is prohibited within the Tijaniya order. Nevertheless, similar to other Sufi orders, Tijani followers cultivate relationships with initiators,

Source: (Osmenda, 2011), (Mourad07, 2015).

Fig. 4: Zawiya and Mausoleum of Sidi Ahmed al-Tijani, Fez, Morocco

akin to a paternal bond. Affiliation is acknowledged through through birth or reciting the litanies of this Sufi order (The Tijaniyya Brotherhood, 2023). Like most of Sufi orders, Tijaniya faces opposition from many Muslims who reject the asserted direct connection between its founder and Prophet Muhammad.

4. Other Sufi orders

Other Sufi Orders in Morocco encompass a diverse array of spiritual paths, each with its distinct practices and teachings. Among these, the Isawiyya, Jilalia, Nasiriyya, Alawiyya, and Karkariya Sufi orders stand out as prominent examples. These orders have established their zawiayas and other institutions engaging in various activities that promote spiritual growth and community cohesion. The presence of these Sufi orders in Morocco adds to the cultural and religious diversity of the nation, weaving a dynamic tapestry of vibrancy across the landscape.

Among the distinctive practices observed in various Sufi orders in Morocco, an intriguing custom involves wearing vibrant attire made from small pieces of diverse materials such as wool or leather. This assemblage of cloth pieces, referred to as "Ruq'aa" in Arabic, gives rise to what is known as "muraqqa'a" clothes, often symbolizing the modest status of those who wear them. The Karkariya Sufi order is notably recognized for adopting this colorful "muraqqa'a," as depicted in Figure 5. According to this order's beliefs, these multicolored clothes not only signify asceticism

Source: (Wikimedia, 2012).

Fig. 5: Colorful clothes of 'muraqqa'a' adopted by the Karkaria order

by emulating the clothing of the impoverished, but it also symbolizes an outward expression and a means of being adorned by the beauty of the concealed Essence, as revealed through the diverse divine names represented by the colors of a dignified and elevated rainbow (Karkariya-Africa).

"Dhikr" which refers to the remembrance of God is one of the common features of the Sufi orders generally. Also, "hadra" is another prevalent practices across the majority of Sufi orders. In Arabic, "hadra حضرة" signifies the concept of being present. Within the Sufi context, this "hadra" alludes to a collective voluntary ritual performed through various practices, coupled with the recitation of their distinct "dhikr" that is specific to each Sufi order. Additional activities conducted during "hadra" gatherings include the praise of Prophet Muhammad, the recitation of the Quran, and collective readings of devotional texts adopted by each Sufi order. Certain orders also incorporate a form of swaying and dancing accompanied by religious chants during these "hadra" sessions. Hence, certain forms of Sufi music and dance have arisen as a result of these rituals. An instance of this unique music is found within the Isawiyya Sufi order in Morocco, where these practices have given birth to a distinctive musical tradition. This musical expression serves to enhance the emotional depth experienced during the recitation of dhikr.

Established in Meknes, Morocco, by Sheikh al-Kamil Mohamed al-Hadi ben Issa (1465-1526), the Isawiyya Sufi order's spiritual principles

Source: (Al-Quity, 2022).

Fig. 6: The Issawa Girls Band, the first women's group for Issawiya songs in Morocco

are rooted in the ancient mystical practices of the Shadhiliyya/Jazuliyya tradition in the 15th century. Interestingly, Isawiyya music and religious chanting evolved through the Isawiyya order to become famous in Morocco. Typically led by groups of men, these musical and chanting performances have recently also been undertaken by women's groups in public settings (Al-Quity, 2022). The image in figure 6 illustrates one of these female Isawiyya singing groups, called "Issawa Girls Band", which is the first women's group for the popular Issawiya songs in Morocco.

IV. Sufi influence in the Moroccan society

In Morocco's history, Sufism stood out for its active and dynamic engagement with society, adopting various roles that encompassed education, guidance, and its positive influence across various domains such as social, economic, and political spheres, imbued with moral values. This educational focus manifested in its contributions to spreading Islam, organizing religious events and group pilgrimages, and fostering unity within the community around shared beliefs. The educational role of Sufism is seen in activities such as Quran memorization, teaching Islamic sciences, establishing Islamic schools and libraries, and religious centers (Al-alamy, 2012).

Source: (Delpha, 2023).

Fig. 7: The Zawiya and Mausoleum of Sidi Bel Abbes in Marrakesh

In terms of social and solidarity efforts, renowned Sufis like Abu al-Abbas al-Sabti exemplified compassion by providing shelter and sustenance, especially in times of crises and epidemics (Al-Tadli, 1997, p. 322). Even after his passing, the zawiya where his mausoleum is situated continues to engage in various charitable endeavors and other religious educational activities in Marrakech, the city where he resided. Figure 7 shows this zawiya.

Sufi leaders played significant roles in maintaining community cohesion, ensuring security, mediating disputes, and safeguarding travel routes. The realm of jihad saw Sufism's call to action against foreign colonization, exemplified by figures like Abu al-Hasan Al-Shazli, revealing Sufism's commitment to both faith and homeland. Moreover, Sufism aligned itself with national leadership, emphasizing the values of loyalty and obedience. This is evident through historical documentation, which cites notable figures endorsing the authority and fondness of rulers (Al-alamy, 2012). This allegiance to the nation's leaders not only reinforced Sufism's function as a uniting influence but also played a vital role in maintaining societal stability and unity.

According to the Ministry of Religious Endowments and Islamic Affairs in Morocco, a total of 7,090 Sufi institutions were identified in the country in 2019 consisting of 1588 zawaya, 5471 shrines, in addition to 31 complexes that encompassed both zawaya and shrines (Moroccan Ministry of Religious Endowments and Islamic Affairs, 2019, p. 24). This data highlights the extensive influence of Sufism in Morocco, as evidenced by the significant number of Sufi institutions, including zawaya, shrines, and complexes. These figures underscore the widespread and diverse activities of Sufism in the country, underscoring its deep integration into

Moroccan society.

For decades, fundamentalist Islamic movements such as Salafism and Wahhabism have exerted a notable influence in Morocco, particularly intensifying their impact since the 1970s. This influence has manifested in the dissemination of extremist propaganda, which has culminated in acts of terror, notably exemplified by the al-Qaida attacks in Casablanca in 2003. In response to these events, King Mohammed VI of Morocco strategically embraced Sufism among the means to combat extremism. A significant step in this direction was his appointment of Ahmed Toufiq, an academic rooted in Sufi traditions, as the Minister for Islamic Affairs. In this role, Toufiq underscores the social and compassionate facets of Sufism within Moroccan culture. Being associated with the Boutchichiyya brotherhood, Toufiq played a pivotal role in establishing the Mohammed VI Institute for the Training of Imams in 2014, a move aimed at fostering a more moderate and empathetic understanding of Islam (Brehmer, 2022). This summarizes how Sufism was embedded into Moroccan society, with the endorsement of the political authorities.

In this context, the Moroccan monarchy has utilized the Zawiya Tijania, a prominent Sufi order, not only in domestic politics but also to strengthen its foreign policy objectives. The Tijani order, which spans North Africa, the Sahel, and West Africa, has played a significant role in revitalizing relations between Morocco and its Francophone West African neighbors. Over the past ten years, Morocco has aimed to rebuild and reestablish connections with the rest of Africa in its foreign policy approach. One of the key motivations behind this effort is the Western Saharan conflict, where Morocco is in opposition to the Polisario liberation movement, backed by Algeria, in a protracted dispute over the rightful governance of the Western Saharan territory (Fakir, 2021, p. 130). Aligned with this dynamic, we cans see that Sufi activities within the Tijani order are serving as a conduit for political objectives in Morocco's foreign relations with Africa.

In a similar context, when certain African nations lent support to the Polisario's claim of sovereignty over Western Sahara, Morocco's 1983 withdrawal from the African Union in protest redirected its foreign policy towards Western powers that held sway over pivotal international negotiation mechanisms. This shift led to a phase of relative disregard for many African partners. Nevertheless, in the past decade, Morocco has adopted a more proactive approach, under the leadership of King Mohammed VI, to foster stronger connections with African counterparts. These initiatives, chiefly focused on investment and economic collaboration, have been augmented by "spiritual diplomacy" exemplified by the Zawiya Tijania, further enhancing Morocco's engagement in the region. Building upon these diplomatic initiatives, the Ministry of Endowments took substantive actions by leveraging Sufism. Particularly noteworthy were the arrangements for "The Sufi Schools Conference" held in Fez in 1986 and the establishment of "The Rabita of Moroccan and Senegalese Ulemas" during the same year, accompanied by other strategic measures that underscored an emphasis on Sufi traditions and collaborative alliances with African scholars (Hmimnat, 2018).

These strategic endeavors highlight the proactive measures Morocco took to address its relative isolation within the African continent but also reflect the nation's astute response to the urgent need for reinvigorating its political and diplomatic engagements. Using the influential tool of Sufism, Morocco demonstrated its commitment to enhancing its presence and its diplomatic ties across the continent. This serves as evidence of Morocco's recognition of the profound influence wielded by Sufism and the essential role it plays in promoting convergence, which extends beyond religious boundaries and contributes to strengthening social cohesion and connections among individuals from diverse backgrounds.

This utilization of Sufism's influence was evident during King Mohammed VI of Morocco's visits to several African countries between 2013 and 2014. During these visits, he proactively interacted with prominent religious leaders and influential Sufi sheikhs, who wield considerable authority in these nations, notably in Senegal, Côte d'Ivoire, and Gabon. In this context, the King held meetings with sheikhs and spiritual leaders from different Tijaniya Sufi lineages, as well as representatives from other Sufi schools, including Al Qadiriya and Al Maridiya (Ministry of Awqaf and Islamic Affairs, 2013). This demonstrated the Moroccan King's commitment to fostering relationships and strengthening connections with religious figures who play a crucial role in their respective communities and religious traditions.

Also, the Boutchichi order is one of the most active Sufi orders in the Moroccan society. It has developed a semi-formal educational system, including a summer program that focuses on religious and spiritual education. This program emphasizes Sufi principles that promote openness, reject radicalization, and discourage extremism. The order's events, particularly the annual conference called "The World Meeting of Sufism," attract elites, especially the youth (Bekkaoui & Larémont, 2011, p. 38).

The Boutchichi order has also engaged with young Moroccan Salafists to promote the virtues of Sufism. Notably, the order supported Morocco's 2011 constitutional revisions and mobilized its adherents to vote in favor of the monarchy, aligning with the Ministry of Religious Endowments and Islamic Affairs' efforts to encourage a yes vote through Friday sermons nationwide. This demonstrated a public and organized endeavor to politically mobilize the order's followers on behalf of the state and the monarchy (Fakir, 2021, p. 130).

The Boutchichi order's strong association with the state bolsters its religious and social identity, as it is currently the most influential order in Morocco. Its proximity to power, pragmatism, organizational capacity, and the extensive network of its followers have shaped its utility to the state. Membership in the order is seen as a means of professional and social advancement, particularly within elite circles, making it a sought-after "social elevator." Prominent members of the Boutchichi order include the Minister of Islamic Affairs, Ahmed Toufiq, his chief of cabinet, Ahmad Qustas, and Ahmed Abaddi, the Secretary General of the Council of Religious Scholars (Bouasria, 2015, p. 165).

These were examples that underscore the significant role of Sufism in Moroccan society. Similar parallels can be drawn between the connections of Sufis with the Moroccan monarchy and the context in Egypt, as previously demonstrated in the third chapter of this book. Similarly, Egyptian Sufis maintained favorable ties with successive Egyptian governments. However, the role of Sufi orders in Morocco holds a broader scope, encompassing diplomatic endeavors and international relations with fellow African nations, setting it apart from its Egyptian counterpart.

■ References

Abun-Nasr, J. (1965). *The Tijaniyya, a Sufi order in the modern world.* London: Oxford University Press.

Al-alamy, T. (2012, 10 16). *The Moroccan Sufism (التصوف المغربي).* Retrieved from Arrabita Almohammadiya-Morocco: https://www.arrabita.ma/blog/التصوف المغربي/#:~:text=%دخول%20التصوف%20لبلاد%20الشخصية, المغرب،%20حيث وقد%20بدأت%20تظهر%20ملامح%20المغرب20

Al-jazeera. (2017, Jan. 19). *Boutchichiya in Morocco.. the love of the "poor" and the blessing of the regime (البودشيشية بالمغرب.. عشق "الفقير" ومباركة النظام).* Retrieved from Al-jazeera: https://www.aljazeera.net/encyclopedia/2017/1/19

Al-Mālikī, A. (2023). *The Shādhilī Way.* Independently published .

Al-Qaderi, A. Q. (1979, Dec. 1). The Qadiriya corner and its religious and social role (الزاوية القادرية ودورها الديني والاجتماعي). *Majalat Dawat Al-haq (مجلة دعوة الحق),* pp. 48-53. Retrieved from Ministry of Endowments and Islamic Affairs of Morocco: https://archive.org/details/Da3wat-AlHaq-Magazine_202/page/n53/mode/2up

Al-Quity, S. (2022, Feb. 22). *In the love of the Prophet.. Women's voices break into the Issawiya song in Morocco.* Retrieved from Al-Jazeera: https://www.aljazeera.net/arts/2021/2/22/نسائية-أصوات-بالمغرب-عيساوة-بنات

Al-Tadli, I. A.-Z. (1997). *Looking upon the men of Sufism and the hagiography of Abi Al-Abbas Al-Sabti {التشوف إلى رجال التصوف وأخبار أبي العباس السبتي}.* (A. Al-Tawfiq, Ed.) Rabat: The College of Arts and Humanities.

Ashmakh, R. (2023, May 24). *Madagh Zawiya at night.* Retrieved from Wikimedia: https://upload.wikimedia.org/wikipedia/commons/f/f3/مساء_مداغ_زاوية.jpg

Badreldin, A. (2014, April 25). *The Crisis of Sufi orders in Morocco (أزمة التصوف الطرائقي في المغرب).* Retrieved from Mominoun Without

Brders for Studies and Researches: mominoun.com/articles/-أزمة-التصوف-#الطرائقي-في-المغرب-1488

Bekkaoui, K., & Larémont, R. R. (2011). Morocco Youth Go Sufi. *Journal of the Middle East and Africa, 2*(3), 31–46. Retrieved from https://www.tandfonline.com/doi/abs/10.1080/21520844.2011.565711

Bouasria, A. (2015). *Sufism and Politics in Morocco: Activism and Dissent.* Oxfordshire: Routledge.

Brehmer, M. (2022, Sep. 19). *Sufism in Morocco: A cure for extremism?* Retrieved from Qantara.de: https://en.qantara.de/content/sufism-in-morocco-a-cure-for-extremism

Britannica, The Editors of Encyclopaedia. (2018, April 10). *Mālikī.* Retrieved from Encyclopedia Britannica: https://www.britannica.com/topic/Maliki-school

Cornell, V. J. (2010). *Realm of the Saint: Power and Authority in Moroccan Sufism.* Austin: University of Texas Press.

Delpha. (2023, July 15). *Zawiya of Sidi Bel Abbes.* Retrieved from Wikipedia: https://en.wikipedia.org/wiki/Zawiya_of_Sidi_Bel_Abbes

El-Resala. (2020, March 4). *Safi: the city of Saints (آسفي: مدينة الأولياء).* Retrieved from El-Resala.com: https://el-ressala.com/آسفي-مدينة-الأولياء/

Encyclopædia Britannica. (n.d.). *Physical features of Morocco.* Retrieved Aug. 11, 2023, from Encyclopædia Britannica,: https://www.britannica.com/place/Morocco/Relief

Euromagreb. (2022, Oct. 4). *Organization of the 17th session of the International Forum of Sufism Under the slogan: "Sufism and the question of action: from the reform of the individual to the construction of society.* Retrieved from Euromagreb: https://euromagreb.com/organisation-de-la-17e-session-du-forum-international-du-soufisme-sous-le-slogan-le-soufisme-et-la-question-de-laction-de-la-reforme-de-lindividu-a-la-construction-de-la-societe/

Fakir, I. (2021, June 7). The Moroccan Monarchy's Political Agenda for Reviving Sufi Orders. In F. Wehrey (Ed.), *Islamic Institutions in Arab States: Mapping the Dynamics of Control, Co-option, and Contention* (pp. 121-134). Washington, DC: Carnegie Endowment International Peace. Retrieved from Carnegie Endowment International Peace: https://carnegieendowment.org/files/202106-IslamicInstitutions-final-updated.pdf

Hammad, K. (2016, Jan. 2). The Boudchichi Order: a critical study. *Official website of Hammad Kabbaj*, pp. http://kabbadj.com/الطريقة-الموقعين/أعلام-مختارات البودشيشية-الصوفية-في كنف-الد/.

Hitti, P. K. (1996). *The Arabs: A Short History*. Washington, D.C.: Regnery Publishing,.

Hmimnat, S. (2018, June 6). *Morocco's Religious 'Soft Power' in Africa: As a Strategy Supporting Morocco's Stretching in Africa.* Retrieved from Moroccan Institute for Policy Analysis: https://mipa.institute/en/5642

Karkariya-Africa. (n.d.). *Muraqa'a, a foundation in the path to Allâh.* Retrieved from Karkariya-Africa: https://karkariya-africa.com/en/the-muraqaa/

Ministry of Awqaf and Islamic Affairs. (2013, March 28). *Activities of His Majesty King Mohammed VI, "the Commander of Believers, during his visits to Senegal, Côte d'Ivoire and Gabon.* Retrieved from The portal of the Ministry of Awqaf and Islamic Affairs: http://www.habous.gov.ma/المؤ-أمير/2865/المؤمنين-إمارة

Mohammed VI Foundation of African Oulema. (2019, Jan. 31). *Shadhili Order* (الطريقة الشاذلية). Retrieved from FM6OA.org: https://www.fm6oa.org/الطريقة-الشـاذليـة/

Moroccan Ministry of Religious Endowments and Islamic Affairs. (2019). *Islamic Affairs.* Rabat: Moroccan Ministry of Religious Endowments and Islamic Affairs. Retrieved from https://www.habous.gov.ma/images/170820_-2019_affaires_islamique/الشؤون الإسلامية/منجزات 2019/2017

pdf

Mourad07. (2015, March 10). *Zaouiya Tidjaniya de Fès: Tombe.* Retrieved from Wikipedia: https://ar.wikipedia.org/wiki/زاوية_سيدي_أحمد_التيجاني#/media/ملف: Zaouiya_Tidjaniya_de_Fès_-_tombe.jpg

Mubarak, Z. (2012). *Islamic Sufism in Literature and Ethics (التصوف الإسلامي في الأدب والأخلاق).* Windsor: Hindawy Foundation.

Office of International Religious Freedom. (2022). *Morocco 2022 International Religious Freedom Report.* Retrieved from U.S. Department of State: https:// www.state.gov/reports/2022-report-on-international-religious-freedom/ morocco/

Osmenda, M. (2011, Jan. 8). *A Mosque Minaret: Mausoleum of Ahmed Tijani.* Retrieved from Wikipedia: https://ar.wikipedia.org/wiki/زاوية_سيدي_أحمد_التيجاني

Rodríguez Mediano, F. (2016). *Ibn Mashīsh, ʿAbd al-Salām.* Retrieved from Encyclopaedia of Islam: https://referenceworks.brillonline.com/entries/ encyclopaedia-of-islam-3/ibn-mashish-abd-al-salam-COM_23907

Saissi, E. (2007, April 29). *Abu Mohamed Saleh (أبو محمد صالح).* Retrieved from Wikipedia: https://ar.wikipedia.org/wiki/أبو_محمد_صالح#/media/ملف:Tombeaucheikh.jpg

Swearingen, W. D., Miller, S. G., & Laroui, A. (2023, Aug. 9). *Morocco: History.* Retrieved from Encyclopedia Britannica: https://www.britannica.com/ place/Morocco/Decline-of-traditional-government-1830-1912

The Editors of Encyclopaedia. (2021, Jun. 22). *Tijāniyyah.* Retrieved from Encyclopedia Britannica: https://www.britannica.com/topic/Tijaniyyah. Accessed 17 August 2023.

The Editors of Encyclopaedia. (2023, Jul. 12). *Abd al-Qādir al-Jīlānī.* Retrieved from Encyclopedia Britannica: https://www.britannica.com/topic/Qadiriyyah

The Tijaniyya Brotherhood. (2023). Retrieved from Wolofresources.org: http:// wolofresources.org/tijaniya.htm

Thibdeau, J. C. (2021). *Sufism in Moroccan Public Life: Teaching Ethics and Performing Piety*. Santa Barbara: University of California.

Tidjania Order. (2020, Oct. 7). *Sheikh Sidi Ahmed Al-Tijani* (الشيخ سيدي أحمد التجاني). Retrieved from The official website of Tidjania order: https://www.tidjania. ma/الشيخ-سيدي-أحمد-التجاني-النشأة-والدرا/

Trimingham, J. S. (1988). *The Sufi Orders in Islam*. Oxford: Oxford University.

Wikimedia. (2012, Dec. 16). *Poor people of the Karkariya Order*. Retrieved from Wikimedia: https://commons.wikimedia.org/wiki/File:3_فقراء_الطريقة_الكركرية.jpg

Conclusion

———

Challenges and Future prospects

The primary objective of this book was to demonstrate the rich diversity and plurality among Muslims, with a particular focus on North Africa. This goal was achieved through the comprehensive exploration presented in the seven chapters that constitute this book. The overarching aim was to challenge and transform the prevailing stereotype about Muslims, which often constrains them to a narrow and homogenous perception oversimplifying their identity as a homogeneous entity with uniform beliefs and perspectives. This objective was achieved by highlighting many diverse dimensions of the Muslim populations across the North African countries.

Through the chapters of this book, the exploration of diversity and plurality within the Muslim population of the North African region was conducted across five representative countries of this geographical area. Starting with Egypt, the Muslim groups constituting the religious fabric of these North African nations exhibited a range of principles, occasionally marked by internal contradictions. Subsequently, Libya emerged as a pertinent case study, exemplifying a pluralistic tribal landscape where multiple tribes coalesce to form the Libyan Muslim community. Transitioning to Tunisia, another layer of diversity was uncovered, underscored by its distinct interpretation of certain Islamic concepts. This unique perspective has contributed to the evolution of how these concepts are applied within contemporary Muslim society. Lastly, the spotlight turned to Morocco, where the multifaceted spectrum of Muslim Sufi groups was explored, offering insights into the mystical facets of Islam.

1. Challenges facing the diversity and plurality among Muslims of North Africa

The pronounced challenge confronting the diversity and plurality observed among North African Muslims lies in the potential for tensions and conflicts that could escalate into perilous situations, carrying repercussions on a global scale. This region, encompassing a segment of the Muslim world that extends across the globe, underscores the interconnectedness of these issues and their broader impact.

The manifestation of these conflicts becomes evident through various instances, such as the case of Islamist groups in Algeria and the prevailing tensions between Sufis and Salafis in some countries like Egypt. These tensions and divisions within the Muslim community can potentially lead to profound repercussions. Thus, these conflicts, if left unaddressed, can escalate over time and tragically evolve into more severe forms. An illustrative case that vividly underscores the gravity of these conflicts is the trajectory of the civilian war in Algeria, spanning from 1991 to 2002, which left a devastating toll with more than a hundred thousand deaths. Moreover, this period of violent turmoil was succeeded by the persistent armed opposition spearheaded by some Islamist militant groups. This sobering example serves as a stark reminder of how internal tensions and ideological disputes can have far-reaching consequences, impacting the social, political, and human fabric of a nation for years to come.

Another compelling instance illustrating the tragic ramifications of these conflicts is the civilian war in Libya. This conflict underwent a deeply distressing transformation, driven by the internal divisions that had been brewing within the nation. The culmination of these divisions was the eruption of a full-scale civil war, a development that became evident in the aftermath of the 2011 revolution. This sobering narrative serves as a poignant reminder of how what may seem to be internal quarrels can, over time, escalate into crises of immense proportions. The role of tribal plurality in fueling this civil war is unmistakable.

When exploring the potential conflicts that could emerge as a result of the diversity and plurality within the Muslim groups and sects of North

Africa, it becomes evident that the historical sectarian divide between the main two Muslim sects, Sunni and Shi'a, is a notable instance. Despite the prevalence of Sunni Muslims among the majority in North Africa, there also exists a Shi'a minority within these countries of the region. This disparity gives rise to critical interrelationships between these two sects, often manifesting in both religious and political contexts. The contentious nature of these relations occasionally surfaces and is even exploited for political purposes.

It is evident that conflicts unfolding in other parts of the Muslim world exert their impact on the situation within the North African region as well. A pertinent example of this phenomenon is observed in the conflict in Syria, which has taken on a distinct sectarian dimension. This conflict is characterized by a Shi'a minority ruling over a Sunni majority, resulting in a complex interplay of religious affiliations. This intricate dynamic extends beyond the geographical confines of Syria, exerting its influence on the interactions between Shi'a and Sunni communities across various Muslim nations, including those situated within the North African region.

An illustrative case that demonstrates the interplay between conflicts in various parts of the Muslim world and their repercussions in the North African region can be observed through the lens of Egypt. In 2013, Egypt experienced a surge in anti-Shi'a sentiments, a trend partly influenced by the reverberations of the ongoing civil war in Syria. Tragically, this escalation culminated in the loss of life for four Shia Muslims, including a prominent Egyptian Shi'a leader, and inflicted injuries upon several others.[1] This unsettling episode underscores the intricate interconnections among sectarian dynamics across the broader Muslim global landscape. It emphasizes how conflicts that arise in one corner of the world can rapidly transmit their consequences to other regions, often exacerbating pre-existing tensions and adding complexity to the intricate tapestry of religious relationships.

There are additional challenges that compound the intricacies of plurality and diversity within the North African region. Among these challenges is the issue of Political Instability, which plagues certain countries in the region. This instability can further worsen pre-existing tensions and provide an avenue for exploiting religious differences for political purposes. The unpredictable nature of politics can intensify divisions and contribute to an environment where religious affiliations are manipulated to gain advantages.

Furthermore, the presence of Extremist Ideologies poses yet another substantial challenge. These ideologies foster radicalization and breed intolerance, potentially undermining the harmony that a diverse society seeks to achieve. It's worth noting that governments within North African countries recognize this challenge and have taken measures to address it.

---

1   For more details in these incidents, see: https://www.bbc.com/news/world-middle-east-23026865

Some governments have chosen to support particular Muslim groups, such as Sufis, as a means of countering these extremist ideologies. By supporting groups that advocate for tolerance and understanding within Islam, they aim to counteract the spread of radical ideas and promote a more inclusive and harmonious religious landscape.

2. Future prospects on the diversity and plurality among Muslims of North Africa

In envisioning the future of the diverse Muslim communities in North Africa, a tapestry of potential prospects emerges, accompanied by a blend of hopes and concerns. This dynamic landscape holds aspirations for increased understanding, coexistence, and shared harmony among its diverse constituents. Yet, in the midst of these aspirations, there also lies a recognition of potential tensions and conflicts that may arise. As we explore the forthcoming possibilities, the desire for unity and the apprehension of challenges shape our exploration of the road ahead.

As this dynamic region navigates the complexities of its religious landscape, a range of avenues present themselves to shape a more inclusive and harmonious future. From interfaith dialogue to educational campaigns, from cultural exchange to fostering representation, the opportunities to cultivate unity among the numerous sects and groups are both diverse and promising. In this part of the conclusion, we will try to delve into some of these potential pathways, exploring how they can contribute to a tapestry that celebrates the richness of diversity while nurturing a sense of belonging and shared purpose among the Muslim communities of North Africa.

Starting with the interfaith dialogue, it becomes evident that initiatives aimed at promoting meaningful conversations and interactions among diverse religious communities can wield a substantial impact on the trajectory of North African societies. By creating platforms for open discourse, these endeavors have the potential to foster a deeper level of understanding and empathy among individuals from different faith traditions. In a region as culturally rich and diverse as North Africa, where a myriad of religious beliefs coexist, the significance of interfaith dialogue cannot be overstated. This approach can facilitate a space where misconceptions can be dispelled, stereotypes shattered, and commonalities celebrated, paving the way for a more harmonious coexistence.

Discussing interfaith dialogue in this context, it's important to clarify that the term doesn't pertain to dialogues between distinct religions. In this case based on the Muslim diversity in North Africa, the focus lies on dialogue occurring within the same religion, specifically among its diverse sects and groups. Thus, within the fabric of Islam in North Africa, where a spectrum of sects and groups coexists, the need for dialogue among these various factions is pronounced. Thus, by promoting dialogue among those different Muslim sects and groups of North Africa, the potential for enhancing mutual understanding and appreciating the diverse ways in which Islam is practiced becomes evident. The conversations sparked by interfaith dialogue can unveil commonalities and shared values that often transcend the denominational lines, fostering a sense of solidarity that can reduce potential tensions and contribute to a cohesive religious landscape.

Within this context, the significance of endeavors such as Sunni–Shi'a dialogue, Sufi–Salafi dialogue, and other encompassing discussions involving diverse Muslim sects is profound. The objective is to initiate conversations that aim for convergence and mutual understanding among these different factions within the broader Muslim community. Through such dialogues, the aspiration is to bridge gaps, clarify misconceptions, and create an environment where diverse perspectives can coexist harmoniously, ultimately contributing to a more unified and cohesive religious landscape.

Another pivotal prospect that holds the promise of fostering a brighter future for the diverse Muslim communities in North Africa revolves around Education and Awareness. Initiating educational campaigns that underscore the significance of unity and the value of respecting diverse beliefs can play a crucial role in cultivating a more harmonious coexistence among Muslims hailing from varying backgrounds. By nurturing a deeper understanding of the shared values that bind this rich tapestry of individuals, these campaigns have the potential to correct misunderstandings and misconceptions. Through education, the foundations for empathy, tolerance, and acceptance can be laid, paving the way for a society where differences are celebrated and celebrated, contributing to a more inclusive and cohesive North African Muslim landscape.

Furthermore, fostering cultural diversity and enhancing mutual understanding can be achieved by actively promoting cultural exchange through comprehensive educational and cultural programs. These initiatives can encompass a range of activities that engage various tribes and groups comprising the North African Muslim community, each stemming from unique backgrounds. By participating in these programs, individuals have the opportunity to gain a deeper appreciation for one another's traditions and values, contributing to a more harmonious coexistence.

Importantly, these programs should not be exclusive to Muslims alone; their scope should extend to include individuals from different religious backgrounds as well. Embracing a more inclusive approach ensures a broader and richer exchange of perspectives, enabling diverse groups to learn from one another. In this way, the promotion of cultural diversity and understanding transcends religious boundaries, fostering an environment where differences are not only acknowledged but also celebrated. Through such endeavors, North African society can move closer to its vision of unity, tolerance, and shared respect among its diverse Muslim and non-Muslim constituents.

■ Author's resume

- Aug. 2022 till present: Director, Center for North African Studies, Institute for Mediterranean Studies, Busan University of Foreign Studies, Busan, South Korea.
- Sep. 2018 till present: HK Assistant Professor, Institute for Mediterranean Studies, Busan University of Foreign Studies, Busan, South Korea.
- 2016: Ph-D degree, Comparative religions, thesis title "Religious Diversity in Contemporary World: Case study of South Korea", Institute of Asian Studies, Zagazig University, Egypt.
- 2013: M.A. degree, Islamic studies, thesis title "Muslim Minority in South Korea: the Present and the Future", Institute for Islamic Studies, Ministry of Higher Education, Cairo, Egypt.
- 1995: B.A. of Political Science, Faculty of Economics & Political Science, Cairo University, Egypt.

Selected publications of the author:

- Basic Arabic Conversations for Koreans (한국인을 위한 기초 아랍어 회화), Busan University of Foreign Studies, 3rd edition, 2023.
- English *translation of the Arabic text "Sicily in Kitāb Ṣūrat al-'Aarḍ (Picture of the Earth)*, Author: Abu al-Qasim Muhammad ibn Hawqal, IMS Booklet, Institute for Mediterranean Studies, BUFS, Aug. 2021.
- *Advanced Arabic Conversations for Koreans (한국인을 위한 고급아랍어 회화)*, Busan University of Foreign Studies, 2017.
- *Refugee Crisis in the Mediterranean*, IMS Booklet, Institute for Mediterranean Studies, Busan University of Foreign Studies, June 2016.
- *Muslim Minority in South Korea: Present and Future*, Center for Asian Studies, Cairo University, 2014.

Diversity and Plurality among Muslims of North Africa

초판인쇄 2023년 12월 4일
초판발행 2023년 12월 4일

지은이 Mona Farouk M. Ahmed
펴낸이 채종준
펴낸곳 한국학술정보(주)
주 소 경기도 파주시 회동길 230(문발동)
전 화 031-908-3181(대표)
팩 스 031-908-3189
홈페이지 http://ebook.kstudy.com
E-mail 출판사업부 publish@kstudy.com
등 록 제일산-115호(2000. 6. 19)

ISBN   979-11-6983-897-9 93930